Professional Practice for Landscape Architects

Nicola Garmory, Rachel Tennant and Clare Winsch

Architectural Press

OXFORD AMSTERDAM BOSTON LONDON NEW YORK PARIS
SAN DIEGO SAN FRANCISCO SINGAPORE SYDNEY TOKYO

Architectural Press
An imprint of Elsevier Science
Linacre House, Jordan Hill, Oxford OX2 8DP
200 Wheeler Road, Burlington MA 01803

First published 2002
Reprinted 2002

British Library Cataloguing in Publication Data
Garmory, Nicola
  Professional practice for landscape architects
  1. Landscape architecture – Great Britain   2. Planning – Law and legislation – Great Britain   3. Landscape architecture – Practice – Great Britain
  I. Title   II. Tennant, Rachel   III. Winsch, Clare
  712.3′0941

Library of Congress Cataloguing in Publication Data
A catalogue record for this book is available from the Library of Congress

ISBN 0 7506 4818X

For information on all Architectural Press publications
visit our website at www.architecturalpress.com

Typeset by J & L Composition Ltd, Filey, North Yorkshire
Printed and bound in Great Britain by Biddles Ltd, *www.biddles.co.uk*

Contents

Professional Practice for Landscape Architects

DATE OF RETURN
UNLESS RECALLED BY LIBRARY

2 5 APR 2006	

PLEASE TAKE GOOD CARE OF THIS BOOK

Introduction

This book covers the fundamental principles of successful professional landscape practice. It provides essential guidance for all levels of landscape architects from students to seasoned practitioners and is a point of reference for everyday professional landscape life.

Topics covered include practice formation and professional ethics; an outline of liability and the law; planning and environmental law; contract administration and procedure.

The book has been designed to incorporate a website, which ensures readers have up-to-date information on changing issues in the current professional environment. The website address referred to throughout this book is www.bh.com/companions/075064818X.

The authors thank John Coultas for his encouragement, support and advice over many years.

Nicola Garmory, Rachel Tennant and Clare Winsch

1 Landscape Practice

Professionalism and Ethics

A professional person is one who belongs to and engages in one of the professions, that is, an occupation requiring intellectual and practical special training, and who is reasonably competent in that occupation. A responsible professional person offers a specialist skill and service for which they are paid.

A professional person enables a client to do something that they are unable to carry out themselves, and a client will employ a professional on the basis of their:

> **• QUALIFICATIONS •**
> Through which they are a member of a profession.

> **• SKILLS •**
> Including their knowledge and experience.

> **•TRUST/ETHICS •**
> A professional will look after the client's interests unlike in a commercial relationship.

The Landscape Institute 协会

A profession has a professional institute or body that protects the status of its membership and governs its members. The Landscape Institute controls who enters the profession, via the objects of the Institute, by safe-guarding the first basis of professionalism, which is your qualification.

The objects of the Landscape Institute, as set out in the Royal Charter of the Landscape Institute (Paragraph 5(1)), are 'to protect, conserve and enhance the natural and built environment for the benefit of the public and':

- To promote the arts and sciences of Landscape Architecture and its several applications.
- To foster and encourage the dissemination of knowledge relating to Landscape Architecture and the promotion of research and education therein.
- To establish, uphold and advance the standards of education, qualification, competence and conduct of those who practice Landscape Architecture as a profession.
- To determine standards and criteria for education training and experience.

The Landscape Institute was granted Royal Charter status in July 1997. The title of 'Landscape Architect' is the professional title now protected by Charter in the UK. This has the following effects:

- Only members and fellows are able to use the protected title of 'Chartered Landscape Architect'.
- Only registered practices can describe their practices as 'Chartered Landscape Architects'.
- Associates and fellows are now 'members' (MLI).
- Graduates become 'associates' but cannot use the letters 'MLI'.
- Branches replace chapters and every member is assigned a branch.
- The Landscape Institute is a statutory government body, consulted on all relevant issues.

Landscape architects are obliged to act in accordance with the requirements of the Landscape Institute's Charter of Incorporation, which defines the professional title of Landscape Architect (Paragraph 5(2)).

The Landscape Institute's Charter of Incorporation: Paragraph 5(2)

- The application of intellectual and analytical skills to the assessment and evaluation of the landscape and its character and the resolution of existing and potential conflicts through the organization of landscape elements, spaces and activities based on sound principles of ecology, horticulture, design, planning, construction and management.
- The planning and design of all types of outdoor and enclosed spaces.

- The determination of policies and planning for existing and future landscapes.
- The appraisal and harmonious integration of development and the built environment into landscapes.
- The conservation, modification and continuing management of the landscapes of town and countryside and sustaining their characteristic features and habitats.
- The promotion of greater knowledge and understanding of materials and technology to enhance the appreciation of and resolution of practical landscape issues and problems.
- The promotion of a better understanding of the principles of and purposes of natural, biological and physical systems affecting or relating to the landscape.

The Landscape Institute's Code of Professional Conduct and Practice (*Refer to website*)

The codes of professional conduct of a professional body are devised to protect the interests of the clients of the profession and to maintain the status of the profession in the eyes of society.

The Landscape Institute controls the standard of work and professional ethics via the Code of Professional Conduct and Practice. Members are governed by and are obliged to conduct themselves in accordance with this Code. The Institute's Professional Performance and Conduct Committee can enforce a breach of the Code of Conduct.

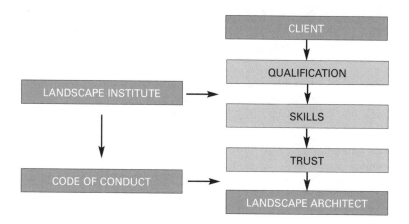

The Landscape Institute updated the Code of Conduct in the summer of 2000. The new code is based on that issued by the Architects Registration Board in 1997 with the aim of achieving a consistent approach to all professional codes.

The new Code consists of four sections including a foreword; introductory clauses, which cover the scope and limit of the Code; the 12 Standards with sub-clauses; and general guidance on interpretation of the Code, legal proceedings, employees and further advice. The Code is seen as 'central to the professional life of a Landscape Architect and a source of ethical guidance and common sense indicator of good practice'. (Reproduced from the *Code of Professional Conduct and Practice*, the Landscape Institute, 2000)

THE STANDARDS OF THE CODE

Standard 1: 'Landscape Architects should at all times act with integrity and avoid any action or situations which are inconsistent with their professional obligations.'

Standard 2: 'Landscape Architects should only undertake professional work for which they are able to provide proper professional and technical competence, and resources.'

Standard 3: 'Landscape Architects should only promote their professional services in a truthful and responsible manner and such promotion shall not be an attempt to subvert professional work from another Chartered Landscape Architect.'

Standard 4: 'Chartered Landscape Architects shall carry out their professional work with care and conscientiously and with proper regard to relevant technical and professional standards.'

Standard 5: 'In agreeing to carry out professional work and in the execution of that work Landscape Architects shall have regard to the interests of those who may be reasonably expected to use or enjoy the product of their work.'

Standard 6: 'Landscape Architects should maintain their professional competence in areas relevant to their professional work and shall provide such educational and training support to less experienced members or students of the profession over which they have a professional or employment responsibility.'

Standard 7: 'Landscape Architects should ensure that their personal and professional finances are managed prudently and shall preserve the security of monies entrusted to their care in the course of practice or business.'

Standard 8: 'Landscape Architects shall not undertake professional work without adequate and appropriate Professional Indemnity Insurance.'

Standard 9: 'Landscape Architects shall organize and manage their professional work responsibly and with integrity and with regard to the interests of their clients.'

Standard 10: 'A Landscape Architect is expected actively and positively to promote the standards set out in these Standards of Conduct and Practice.'

Standard 11: 'A Landscape Architect is expected actively and positively to promote and further the aims and objectives of the Landscape Institute, as set down in its Charter, and to contribute to the work and activities of the Institute.'

Standard 12: 'Complaints concerning professional work of Landscape Architects or their practice or business should be dealt with promptly and appropriately.'

The Landscape Architect's Responsibilities and Obligations

The Landscape Institute's Charter of Incorporation and Code of Professional Conduct and Practice set out the parameters of landscape architects' professional obligations and their responsibilities.

A landscape architect has a responsibility to the environment, society at large, the client, the landscape profession, their own organization/colleagues, and also to other professionals and contracting organizations. These responsibilities are expressed through the undertaking or provision of:

• PROFESSIONAL SKILLS •

• ADVICE/INFORMATION •

• LEGAL KNOWLEDGE •

• OFFICE AND PROJECT MANAGEMENT •

• CONTINUING PROFESSIONAL DEVELOPMENT •

A landscape architect has a responsibility to the client as:

A Skilled Professional Person

- 'The landscape architect will use reasonable skill, care and diligence in fulfilling their services to the client in accordance with the <u>normal</u> standards of the profession.' (*The Landscape Consultant's Appointment: Clause 3.2 Duty of Care. Refer also to Standard 4.2 of the Code of Professional Conduct and Practice: 'LA's shall perform with due skill, care and diligence.'*)
- Landscape architects are obliged to conduct themselves in accordance with the Code of Professional Conduct, which governs the standard of professional conduct and self-discipline required of Members of the Landscape Institute.

A Responsible Agent

- The landscape architect is the client's representative and will act on behalf of the client on matters set out in the terms of their appointment. In this capacity, the landscape architect must act in the client's interest and must always remember that the acts done by him on behalf of the client will be deemed to be the acts of the client.

A Quasi-Arbitrator/Arbiter

- The landscape architect will be impartial in administering the terms of a contract between client and contractor. Under the JCLI conditions of contract, the landscape architect as contract administrator is named as Agent, which allows for a quasi-judicial function in resolving issues on a fair and reasonable basis.

Forms of Organization

• PUBLIC SECTOR •

• PRIVATE SECTOR •

The Public Sector

Landscape architects can practice in the public sector in variety of ways but local authorities continue to be the main source of employment. The main forms of public sector organization are:

> **• CENTRAL GOVERNMENT •**
>
> Department of Transport Local Government and the Regions (DTLR), National Assembly for Wales (NAW), Scottish Executive, Northern Ireland Department

> **• CENTRAL GOVERNMENT AGENCIES •**
>
> Forestry Authority and Countryside Agencies

> **• LOCAL GOVERNMENT/AUTHORITY •**
>
> Councils

Local Authority Structure

Local Government Act confers on all local authorities power to arrange for any of its functions to be discharged by a committee, subcommittee or an officer. All local authorities conduct their affairs by a committee system. Committees consisting of elected councillors are entrusted with specified functions of the council e.g. planning committee, finance committee.

The client in the public sector is the council committee e.g. planning, housing, leisure and recreation. As with private clients, these public ones decide priorities and allocate funds. Their approval is necessary before work begins. A committee representative, usually the chairman, also signs tenders once they have been received back from tenderers.

Decisions are recommended to the council or to the relevant committee usually by the corresponding department's director. If approved, it is then the duty of the appropriate officer (e.g. landscape architect) of the council to implement the decision, satisfy the committee's requirements and report back to them if required to do so (e.g. by Standing Order).

Compulsory Competitive Tendering (CCT) and Best Value

The 1980 Local Government Planning and Land Act introduced the idea that direct labour sections involved in construction and maintenance of local authority buildings had to tender for this work in competition with private construction companies.

Similar legislation came into force in 1992 to cover maintenance of council land, sport and recreational facilities, and professional and 'white-collar' services including housing management, financial services and design.

The Government in 1997 heralded 'Best Value' as an alternative to CCT. Best Value is even more challenging than CCT because 100 per cent of council services and everyone in the council – all council employees and Elected Members – are directly involved. Moreover, although tendering is no longer compulsory, councils still have to consider competition and 'alternative forms of service delivery'. This may include Voluntary Competitive Tendering (VCT), Private Finance Initiative (PFI) Trusts and other forms of partnership.

The Private Sector

The main forms of practice or organization in the private sector are:

• PARTNERSHIPS •
• COMPANIES •
• SOLE TRADERS/PRACTITIONERS •

Partnerships

This is the most common form of association because it is a form of contract i.e. it is legally binding and it has the benefits of mutual support and combined resources. A partnership is not a separate legal entity from its partners (except in Scotland), therefore when a third party enters a legal agreement with a partnership, they do so with the partners themselves.

A partnership is less formal than a company, with freedom of action and privacy of its affairs. However, it is subject to unlimited liability with personal assets at risk; it has limited powers to borrow money and the taxation position is complex.

The principal elements in understanding partnerships are:

1 RECOGNITION OF PARTNERSHIPS.
2 PARTNERSHIP AGREEMENTS.
3 TYPES OF PARTNERSHIPS.
4 MANAGEMENT AND TYPES OF PARTNERS.
5 FINANCE/ACCOUNTS.
6 SIZE OF PARTNERSHIPS.
7 LIABILITIES.
8 DISSOLUTION OF PARTNERSHIPS.

Recognition of a Partnership

The essentials for recognition of a partnership are contained in the Partnership Act 1890, which states that a partnership is a *'Relationship which subsists between a collection of persons carrying on a business in common with a view to profit'*.

Sharing of facilities does not mean two people practise in common, but shared ownership of property and sharing of net profits are evidence of the existence of a partnership.

Partnership Agreements

Obligations are borne by the partners as individuals and hence it is very important that their rights and duties are set out in a written partnership agreement. In the absence of this the provisions set out in the Partnership Act 1890 will apply:

> - Property brought into the firm or bought with the firm's funds is partnership property.
> - Profits and losses will be shared equally.
> - Every partner is entitled to take part in the management of the business.
> - No partner is entitled to a salary.
> - No change can be made to the business of the firm.
> - No new partners may be introduced and no partner may be expelled by the other partners.

Types of Partnerships

Unlimited (liability) partnerships are most common and controlled by the Limitations Act 1980. Limited (liability) partnerships are not common because of the many disadvantages, and also following the simplification of the Companies Act 1985 and 1989. They are governed by the Limited Partnership Act 1907.

Management/Types of Partner

Management is by the partners. There is no distinction between junior and senior partners except to decide how to share profits. However, under the Limited Partnership Act 1907, some partners may have their liability limited by agreement with other members of the partnership.

The term 'salaried partner' may appear not to have any legal standing. However, a salaried partner will have the rights and be subject to the duties contained in the Partnership Act unless the partnership agreement expressly provides that the salaried partner remains an employee of the firm. This should include for indemnity provided by the true partners against liability to a third party.

The title 'Associate' is not referred to in the Partnership Act and it has no meaning in law. The title is often used to retain important members of staff while preventing them having any real responsibility or appreciable share of the profits.

Finance/Accounts

Partnerships are liable to income tax on their profits whether they are drawn at or left in the practice. The partnership's profits are shared equally, or as stated in the partnership agreement and no audit is required of the business accounts.

Size

Partnerships are restricted in size. The Companies Act 1985 restricts the formation of partnerships consisting of more than twenty partners. However, the Partnerships (Unrestricted Size) No. 14 Regulations 2000 exempt from that prohibition partnerships formed for the purpose of activities listed in the schedule to the Regulations (including Surveying, Estate Management, Land Use Appraisal, Planning and Development) or consisting of members of the RICS.

Liabilities – Unlimited Partnership

In addition to all their normal individual liabilities, each partner has added responsibilities as a member of a partnership. The nature of the liability for the contract debts and torts (including professional negligence) is defined by sections 9 and 12 of the Partnership Act and is summed up:

- Every partner is an agent of the firm.
- If a partnership is sued a partner can be proceeded against 'jointly and severally' i.e. singly/together.
- Partners are jointly liable for a partnership's contract debt, in the absence of agreement to the contrary. (Each partner is bound to contribute to the debts in proportion to his share of the profits. This may be to the whole extent of his property.)
- Partners are jointly and severally liable for the partnership's torts (including negligence) and this cannot be avoided by agreement.
- Partners are jointly and severally liable for the partnership's contract debts if they have expressly agreed to be so liable.
- The estate of a deceased partner is also severally liable for the partnership's contracts, subject to the prior payment of his or her private debts.
- Partners are not liable for the criminal actions of other partners unless they contributed to them or had knowledge of them.
- A new partner entering a firm does not normally become liable for debts, obligations or wrongs incurred or committed before his entry. However, if a partner retires or dies he or his estate will still be liable for debts or obligations incurred before his retirement.

Dissolution of a Partnership

Partnerships can be dissolved or ended in a variety of ways:

- If no time is fixed for the duration of a partnership it is termed a partnership at will, and may be dissolved at the insistence of any partner.
- At the end of a fixed term, if it has been so set up (e.g. a specific commission or for ten years).
- By a court order on the grounds of insanity, incapacity, misconduct of a partner or of the hopeless state of the business.
- If any partner becomes bankrupt, or if there is a change in the partners (death, retirement or resignation) or by the joining of a new partner (new partnership).

Companies

The principal elements in understanding companies are:

1 FORMATION.
2 MANAGEMENT.
3 TYPES OF COMPANY.
4 FINANCE/ACCOUNTS.
5 SIZE.
6 LIABILITIES.
7 DISSOLUTION.

Formation of Companies

A company can be formed in three ways:

- By Royal Charter.
- By Special Act of Parliament.
- By registration under the Companies Acts 1985 and 1989.

Registration under the Companies Act is the most common. The Registrar of Companies will issue a Certificate of Incorporation and give the company a registered number. Without a certificate a company does not exist in law and cannot do business.

Management

A company is controlled by the Companies Acts 1985/1989, which covers its formation and operation. It is owned by its members or shareholders and is governed by its directors or managing director with the supervision of its shareholders.

A company is a distinct and separate entity in law from its members and directors. It can own property, sue and be sued, and enter into contract in its own right. The company continues whoever leaves or joins; it is not affected by the death, bankruptcy or retirement of a shareholder or of a director or other employee.

Types of Company

Two types of company exist; these are limited liability or unlimited liability companies.

Limited Liability or Unlimited Liability Companies

- Limited liability companies are where the shareholders' liabilities are limited to the amount unpaid on their shares. Shareholders may have different interests also e.g. 40 per cent and 20 per cent, therefore their liability and profits will be different. Companies can also be limited by guarantee where shareholders are liable as guarantors for an amount set out in the memorandum in the event of a company being wound up.
- Unlimited liability companies are very unusual. The liability of shareholders generally arises on the winding up of the company and is unlimited, although it may be limited by agreement on entering into transactions and creditors.

Companies whether limited or unlimited may be either public or private.

Public and Private Companies

- A public company is the only sort of company that is permitted to offer its shares to the public and only companies with a certain nominal share capital may be a Public Limited Company (PLC).
- Reasons for flotation on the Stock Exchange, apart from the raising of finance, include the provision of evidence of the standing of the practice, improved efficiency from the necessary disciplined management and the ability to acquire other businesses to widen capabilities.
- A number of large multidisciplinary environmental practices are now PLC but in general a smaller practice will form a private company and probably the individuals who would otherwise be partners will be the directors and also the shareholders.

Accounts/Finance

Profits are distributed among shareholders in accordance with the rights attached to their shares and directors and employees are paid salaries out of the profits of companies, which are tax deducted. Accounts must be audited and filed at Companies House.

Size

The number of shareholders that a company may have is unlimited.

Liabilities of Shareholders

Companies are distinct and separate entities in law. On this basis the liability of shareholders differs from partners in a partnership.

- Shareholders are not liable personally for the torts or obligations incurred by the company or by other shareholders (other than in tort for their own negligence).
- Shareholders are only liable for the debts of the company to the amount unpaid on their shares if the company is limited.
- Shareholders are fully liable for torts and obligations if the company is unlimited *only* on the winding up of the company, otherwise it rests with the company itself.
- If a company is dissolved by winding up, both members and past members (within the past twelve months) will be liable to contribute towards the assets of a company so it can meet its liabilities.

Liabilities of Directors

Directors are normally given the power to manage the company under the ultimate supervision of shareholders and therefore their liabilities are more limited than those of shareholders.

- Directors are not servants/agents of the company but they are liable for their own torts.
- Directors are only allowed remuneration specified in the articles/memorandum.
- A director owes the company a duty of loyalty and faith and must exercise reasonable care in the conduct of business.
- Directors must prepare annual accounts and report on the company's finances/dividend. Companies are audited annually and the audit, report and accounts must be filed with the Register of Companies for public inspection.
- Directors must hold an annual general meeting.

Dissolution of a Company

Companies can be dissolved in the following ways:

- Winding up/liquidation, which is either voluntary or compulsory. Once wound up no judgement may be forced against it.
- By being struck off the register, which will occur when the company is no longer carrying on business. Companies may seek this form of dissolution to save the cost of a formal liquidation.

Companies and Partnership - Key Differences *(Refer to website)*

Sole Principal

Sole practitioners have considerable freedom in the running of their business:

- No formal documentation required for setting up/constitution.
- No legal requirements regarding form of accounts, annual returns (except for Inland Revenue) or statutory books.
- No restrictions on financial drawings.

Against this are set:

- All business and personal assets are at risk.
- There is no legal continuity on death.

Other Forms of Association/Collaboration

Regardless of whether they are practising as partnerships, companies or co-operatives, practices may join forces in various forms of collaboration. This provides for an increased availability of skills and resources while retaining identity and a measure of independence. Such arrangements contrast with the more usual situation where consultants are appointed by the client on the architect's advice and are answerable individually to the client.

- GROUP PRACTICES -

- CONSORTIA -

• CO-OPERATIVES •

•TRUSTS •

Group Practices

Individual private firms of one profession, under various forms of agreement, may be grouped for their mutual benefit and to give better service while each retains some independence e.g.:

•Association of Individual Firms •
Beyond agreeing to a division of overheads and expenses they retain the profits of the individual firms and their normal responsibility to their respective clients.

• Co-ordinated Groups •
For large jobs work can be undertaken by two or more firms with one of them appointed to co-ordinate the activities of the others. The co-ordinating firm is solely liable to the client, but the individual firms are still liable to the co-ordinating firm for acts committed in their area of activity.

Consortia

In law consortia are little different from group practices. The term normally implies the association of firms and different professional skills acting as one for carrying out projects jointly yet retaining their separate identity and each with their own responsibility to the client.

Co-operatives

A co-operative is a method of working rather than a form of practice. It is based on a commitment to the principles of co-operative working and collective decision making. Liability, capital and valuations of the business and members' capital should be clearly defined. A co-operative can be registered either as a company under the Companies Act or as a society with the Register of Friendly Societies under the Industrial and Provident Societies Acts 1965–75. It can be carried out through a promoting body such as the Co-operative Union Industrial Common Ownership Movement (ICOM rules).

Trusts

The key principles of trusts are that they:

- Are non-profit-making organizations.
- Have a board of trustees (normally with other business interests).
- Depend on sponsorship i.e. charity, central government or local funding.
- Are not taxed.
- Have employees.
- Must disclose accounts as per a limited company to the Register of Companies for inspection by the public.

Establishing a Private Practice

The principal elements to be considered when establishing a private practice are:

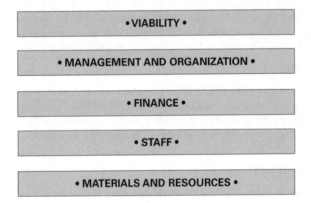

- •VIABILITY•
- • MANAGEMENT AND ORGANIZATION •
- • FINANCE •
- • STAFF •
- • MATERIALS AND RESOURCES •

Viability

The viability of a practice requires to be established and this can be achieved through:

- Market sector research and targeting.
- Competitor research.
- Professional or government advisory services. (The Landscape Institute offers advice and information on setting up in private practice.)
- Preparation of a business plan.

Management and Organization

A number of principles require to be established and organization systems set up:

Decide the Form of Practice

- Partnerships.
- Companies.
- Sole trader or other.

Comply with Statutes and Regulations

- Companies Act 1989: register company name and arrange for auditing of accounts.
- Partnership Act 1890: set up partnership agreement.
- Inland Revenue: register for PAYE and tax.
- HM Customs and Excise: register for VAT contributions.
- Contributions Agency: register for National Insurance Contributions.
- Rates: register with local authority for assessment of rates.
- Employment Act 1980, Employment Rights Act 1996 (rev. 1998) and Employment Relations Act 1999 and current European Community Work Directive and corresponding UK Acts of Parliament: staff employment.
- Offices, Shops and Railway Premises Act 1963, Health and Safety at Work Act 1974 and Health and Safety Information for Employees 1989: health and safety.
- Register with the Landscape Institute to obtain benefits e.g. advertising.

Take out Appropriate Insurances

- Professional indemnity insurance.
- Building and contents insurance.
- Employers' liability insurance against personal accidents to staff.
- Occupier's liability insurance against personal accidents to visitors.
- Other insurances: private medical insurance, pensions, life assurance, crossover insurance, motor insurance.

Set up Office Quality Management Systems

- Quality manual.
- Quality policy.
- Auditing systems.

Finance

Options for raising finance and setting up financial control systems within the office should be considered and initiated:

Raising Money
- Personal savings.
- Bank loan (business plan required).

Establish a Bankbook System
- Records incoming money (fees and expenses) and outgoing money (salaries, overheads and direct expenses).
- Balances the end of the month account with the bank statement.
- Used by the accountant to prepare the annual accounts.

Cash Flow Forecast for Long-Term Financial Planning
- Monthly forecast of fee income.
- Monthly summary of expenditure.
- Forecast of annual fee income and expenditure.
- Profit and loss ratio.

Annual Statement of Accounts and Balance Sheet
Produced (normally by the practice accountant) for:
- Annual accounts audit.
- Tax purposes.
- Annual practice forecasting.

Consultant and Staff Appointment

Consultants
Consultants are external professionals who are essential for the management of the practice. They will include a bank manager, solicitor and accountant.

Internal staff
The appointment of internal staff will depend on the size of the practice. These will usually consist of administrative and professional (junior and senior) staff. Staff recruitment requires the practice to:

Staff Appointment
- Prepare a person and job description.
- Advertise (internally/externally) or through word of mouth.

- Interview.
- Appoint and set up contract of employment.
- Arrange for CPD and training.

Materials and resources
The following list is not exhaustive but will be dependent on the size of the practice.

Materials and Resources
- Office space.
- Office transport.
- Office furniture.
- Computers, telephones, fax, email etc.
- General office materials and stationery.

Appointment of a Landscape Consultant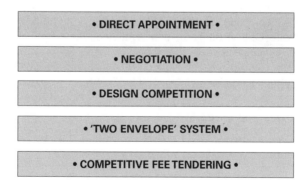

There are various ways in which a landscape consultant may be commissioned. The Landscape Institute's *Guide to Procedure for Competitive Tendering* outlines the alternatives that are suited to particular circumstances:

> • DIRECT APPOINTMENT •

> • NEGOTIATION •

> • DESIGN COMPETITION •

> • 'TWO ENVELOPE' SYSTEM •

> • COMPETITIVE FEE TENDERING •

Direct Appointment

Landscape architects can discuss a potential appointment with a prospective client without obligation. Examples of previous work and/or the individuality of design approaches by practices can be ascertained by a client in order to consider the practice suitability. Many clients build an established working relationship with one or more practices to their mutual benefit.

Negotiation

On large or extended commissions clients can negotiate with one or more practices to obtain the most favourable fee agreement appropriate to the commission. Discussion between client and landscape architect on the particular requirements of the project enables the consultants to tailor the brief and fee basis to mutual advantage.

Design competition

Design competitions are a way of discovering the range of design options available on major projects. To enable a consultant to be selected on the basis of a design competition or technical proposal the client has to ensure adequate information is available to competitors including the basis of remuneration. The criteria and methods used to assess and select from the competition entries must be determined in advance by the client e.g. on the basis of the design or on the fee proposal.

'Two Envelope' System

The 'Two Envelope' system is a method used to evaluate the quality of proposals and the fee tenders at the same time.

Each shortlisted consultant submits a design or technical proposal with a separate sealed fee tender; the client opens all proposals and after evaluation ranks them in preferred order, endorsing the fee tender envelopes with this ranking. The fee tender envelope of the first choice tenderer is then opened and the commission is awarded unless the fee is unacceptable. Only if the fee is unacceptable is the second choice tenderer's fee envelope opened, and so on.

When the commission is awarded, all remaining fee envelopes are returned unopened to the unsuccessful tenderers.

Competitive Fee Tendering

When fee competition is used to select a consultant, the client prepares a shortlist of fully acceptable consultants, by:

> • Pre-Tender Qualification •
> • Known Practices •
> •The Nomination Procedure •

The number of consultants on the shortlist is determined by the project size and will usually range from three to six. In order to invite bids the client prepares a full brief and full project definition. A suitable basis for this process is set out in the Landscape Institute's *Guide to Procedure for Competitive Tendering.*

Approach and Offer of Work: Factors to be Considered by the Landscape Architect

When first approached by a client to undertake work the landscape architect should consider certain factors before accepting/undertaking a commission:

> **• Competence •**
> Whether the landscape architect has relevant experience and is competent to deal with the type of work required.

> **• Commitments •**
> Whether present commitments will permit the landscape architect to devote adequate time and staff to the work.

> **• Finance •**
> Whether the office can carry the job financially.

> **•The Client •**
> The standing and integrity of the client.

Acceptance and Confirmation of Appointment

Acceptance and confirmation of appointment can be made in the following ways:

> **•VERBAL AGREEMENT •**
> (Valid only under Scots law)

> **• UNDER SEAL •**

> **• EXCHANGE OF LETTERS •**

> **• MEMORANDUM OF AGREEMENT •**

Under Seal

This is a formal document drawn up by lawyers detailing the requirements of the client as the first party and the manner in which the professional will undertake and discharge his duties as second party. It is signed, witnessed, sealed and embossed. It is used mainly by large organizations for contracts involving large sums of money e.g. government contracts.

Exchange of Letters

Written formal offer to the client setting out the terms of appointment and other relevant information and asking for confirmation to proceed. Information should clearly set out:

RELEVANT INFORMATION
- Project description and location.
- Scope of services.
- Additional or unusual services.
- Conditions of appointment.
- Fees and expenses.
- Other consultants'/professionals' appointments.
- Site staff.
- Adjudication/arbitration.

Memorandum of Agreement

Misunderstandings may arise from exchange of letters. The Landscape Institute recommends using their Standard Memorandum of Agreement and Schedule of Services and Fees as contained within *The Landscape Consultant's Appointment* as well as issuing the client with a copy of the document itself.

A letter or memorandum of agreement should be sent by registered post or recorded delivery as, should litigation arise, it may be necessary to produce evidence of the client's receipt. *NB The Landscape Institute's Code of Professional Conduct and Practice requires you to agree your terms and conditions with the client in writing (Standard 9).*

Implications of an Agreement between the landscape architect and the client

Once there has been an agreed acceptance and confirmation it signifies the commencement of a contractual relationship. This is reinforced by an assurance of special professional competence and the Code of Professional Conduct of the Institute.

If this relationship breaks down and the contract is breached because there is a failure of either party to perform in accordance with their agreement then the law will give remedy and redress can be sought through the courts. (*Refer to Chapter 2 Liability and the Law.*)

The Landscape Institute's *The Landscape Consultant's Appointment*

History

The Landscape Consultant's Appointment was first issued in 1988 by the Landscape Institute. Its predecessor, *The Conditions of Engagement and Professional Charges*, was withdrawn by the Office of Fair Trading in 1984 under the Restrictive Trade Practices Act 1976 because of the detailed formulae it contained for calculating fees.

The aim of the new document is to ensure that the landscape consultant and the client achieve a clear understanding of the services required by the client and that the conditions concerning the provision of these services are clearly defined.

The document was revised in May 1998 as a result of the Housing Grants, Construction and Regeneration Act 1996, which came into force in April 1998. The Act covers architectural, design and surveying work in relation to construction operations. The Act makes provision for adjudication in the case of disputes, payments, and outlaws 'pay when paid' clauses.

All contracts signed after the Act came into force are subject to these provisions. If the contract itself does not say how this is to be done then the provisions set out in the 'Scheme for Construction Contracts' 1998 will apply automatically. *The Landscape Consultant's Appointment* has now incorporated adjudication and payment within its revised version.

The document comprises:

•THE MEMORANDUM OF AGREEMENT •

• APPENDIX 1 •
THE LANDSCAPE CONSULTANT'S APPOINTMENT
Part 1: The Landscape Consultant's Services
Part 2: Other Services
Part 3: Conditions of Appointment

• APPENDIX 2 •
SCHEDULE OF SERVICES AND FEES

The Memorandum of Agreement

The Landscape Institute advises its members to use the Memorandum of Agreement and the Schedule of Services and Fees to prepare formal agreements with clients to prevent uncertainties occurring for either of both parties as the commission progresses. The Memorandum ensures that the agreement covers the terms of the commission, the scope of the services, the allocation of responsibilities and any limitation of liability, the payment of fees including the rates and method of calculations, and the provision for termination.

Memorandum of Agreement: points to note

- Places a duty on landscape consultant to provide invoices to client in instalments/dates as specified in the schedule. The date of receipt (2 days after posting) of the invoice is the date the fees are due by the client.
- Places a duty on client to acknowledge receipt of invoice, no later than 5 days after receipt, to landscape consultant and specify amount to be paid and the basis of calculation.
- The final date for payment after sum is due is written into the agreement as 7 days (or other as specified).
- Notice for withholding payment has to be given within 7 days before the final date for payment.
- NB The Late Payments of Commercial Debts (Interest) Act 1998 came into force in November 1998. It covers commercial contracts for the supply of goods or services where the supplier is a 'small business' and the purchaser is a 'large business' or UK public authority. The rate of interest has been set at 8 per cent above base rate.

The Landscape Consultant's Appointment: Appendix 1

Part 1: The Landscape Consultant's Services
This describes the preliminary and standard services that a landscape consultant would undertake after accepting a commission and covers design, construction and management, stages A–L, Inception to Completion. These services are then subdivided into work stages. Not all will apply to each commission.

Part 2: Other Services
Part 2 describes the services that are provided outside the design, construction and management process and augments the preliminary and standard services, such as public inquiries, environmental impact assessments, landscape planning, landscape appraisal and evaluation and also other consultants' services.

Part 3: Conditions of Appointment

This describes the conditions that normally apply when a landscape consultant is appointed, from landscape consultant's duty of care: project control, appointment of other consultants, liabilities, termination, adjudication and requirements under CDM Regulations.

Conditions of Appointment: points to note

- **Cl 3.2: The landscape consultant's duty is defined:**
  'The landscape consultant will use reasonable skill, care and diligence in accordance with the normal standards of the profession.'
- **Cl 3.4: The landscape consultant's authority is defined:**
  'The landscape consultant will act on behalf of the client in the matters set out or implied in the landscape consultants appointment . . . '
- **Cl 3.12: Sub-consultant's liability is set out:**
  'Where a consultant is appointed under 3.10 the landscape consultant shall not be held liable for the consultant's work . . . '
- **Cl 3.15: The contractor's responsibility is defined:**
  'The client will employ a contractor under a separate agreement to undertake construction or other works not undertaken by the landscape consultant. The client will hold the contractor and not the landscape consultant responsible for the contractor's operational methods and for the proper execution of the works.'
- **Cl 3.20: Copyright** (also covered under Cl 2.29 and 2.2.10).
- **The client's obligation is also defined in the Introduction:**
  'They must provide adequate information on the project, site and budget and fully understand and approve the landscape consultants proposals . . . '

Schedule of Services and Fees: Appendix 2

Names the parties and the project; refers to the memorandum of agreement; covers the services and specialist conditions that apply and details the method of charging fees, stage payments, expenses and disbursements.

Schedule of Services and Fees: points to note

- Lump sum payments are defined as a single figure.
- Time charge fees allow a detailed breakdown of hourly rates.
- Interim payments allowed for time charge and percentage fees.
- Expenses and disbursements are clearly defined.

Calculating and Charging Professional Fees

The Landscape Institute's Engaging a Landscape Consultant: Guidance for Clients on Fees

In August 1996 the Landscape Institute Practice Committee produced a fee guidance supplement with the aim of promoting the principle of quality balanced with price in providing the best value for money. The booklet is divided into three sections and has attached tables, a fee graph and examples. The document supersedes *The Conditions of Engagement and Professional Charges 1984* and supplements the information and guidance contained within *The Landscape Consultant's Appointment* and the *Guide to Procedure for Comprehensive Tendering*.

Methods of charging fees and expenses

There are three common methods of charging fees:

> **• PERCENTAGE FEES •**
> **• TIME CHARGES •**
> **• LUMP SUMS •**

Other methods exist and include Ceiling Figure, Retainer, Unit Price Fees, Incentive Fees and Betterment Fees but the principal methods are described in detail below.

Percentage Fees

These are fees expressed as a percentage of the total construction cost of the landscape contract or subcontract. Before fees can be calculated both client and landscape architect must establish the services to be provided, the approximate construction budget and the nature of the work e.g. hard or soft landscape or combined; main or subcontract; phasing. Subcontract costs should include an apportionment of main contractors' attendance, preliminaries, profit allowance and fluctuations.

Percentage fees are best used for straightforward landscape projects where the standard services (Stages C–L) are to be used.

Percentage Fees

Available data

- *Engaging a Landscape Consultant: Guidance for Clients on Fees* contains a fee graph, which shows four curves as a range of percentage fees at varied complexity ratings for works of £20 000 and above. This indicates the fee costs that may be incurred by the client for landscape consultants' basic services expressed as percentages of the contract sum. Lower fee percentages may be expected with higher contract sums and vice versa. Projects below the £20 000 threshold should be agreed on a time charge or lump sum fee basis.

- Four different classifications of landscape work are identified depending on degrees of complexity. The four curves on the fee graph correspond to these four classifications and show the nominal percentage fee curve (complexity rating 1) and three other curves (rating 2–4).

NB The graphs are indicative only and are intended to act as a guide.

How applied

- Conventionally on the latest approved revision of the budget until the contract is let and then on the contract sum until the total construction cost is established.

Advantages

- If the budget/tender price is high the consultant will achieve a high fee.

Disadvantages

- A method vulnerable to market forces and their influence on contractors' tendering. If the tender figure is lower than estimated the consultant loses out.
- Working to an agreed figure means cost control is important. There is no flexibility and if the landscape architect budgets incorrectly he loses money.

Time Charges

Time charge fees are when all time expended on the project by principal and technical staff is charged at previously agreed rates, revised at stated intervals.

Time charge fees are best used where the scope of work cannot reasonably be foreseen or where services cannot be related to the amount of landscape construction costs. Additional or varied services on an otherwise basic service, open-ended or protracted planning negotiations are examples where time charges are appropriate.

Time Charges

How applied

- The rates should be calculated in advance for individuals within the office or bands of staff e.g.: principals; associates; senior professionals; junior professionals; technicians.
- The charge-out rate will depend on each individual's wage plus overheads. Often 2.5–3.0 × salary, it should also include a method of revision to reflect subsequent changes in salaries and costs. The time of secretarial and administration staff is not usually charged, but there

are times when it should be e.g. when staff are directly engaged to do semi-technical work on a specific project.

Advantages
- The landscape architect is paid for all the hours worked on the project, including work not anticipated at the outset or abortive work.
- The client pays only for the work done (as opposed to fees as a percentage of the contract sum regardless of how much work the consultant is involved in).

Disadvantages
- From the client's point of view, this method of charging may seem open ended, with uncertainty regarding his total financial commitment until the job is complete.
- It also may seem that the landscape architect has no incentive to work efficiently.
- It is advisable to keep the client informed on the progress of time-charged work, and to agree a figure that is not to be exceeded without prior permission.

Lump Sum Fees

Lump sum fees are when a total sum of money is agreed for a defined package of services. Lump sums are common where the scope of work can be clearly defined from the outset. It is necessary to define the parameters of services i.e. time, project size and cost, where applicable so that if these are varied by more than the stated amount the lump sum itself may be varied. It is unwise to agree a lump sum with no provision for variation except in the case of a highly focused service to be undertaken over a very short period.

Lump Sum Fees

How applied
- At agreed payment intervals and at agreed proportions.
- Time charges are often converted to lump sums when the project becomes sufficiently defined.
- Percentage fees may similarly be converted to lump sums when a firm budget or contract sum is known.

Advantages
- The limit of spend is known by both parties.

Disadvantages
- A lump sum is a risk. If anything goes wrong the practice may lose money yet have no justification for revision of the sum.

Methods of Charging Expenses and Disbursements

The consultant's direct expenses to carry out the job can be calculated and recharged to the client. Recoverable expenses usually include reproduction or purchase costs of all documents, hotel and travelling expenses and rental and hire charges for specialized equipment.

Disbursements are charges properly borne by the client. Examples of disbursements are planning application fees; expenses incurred in advertising for tender and resident site staff; and any fees and charges for specialist professional advice, including legal advice, which have been incurred by the landscape architect with the specific authority of the client.

Expenses can be recovered in a number of ways:

• AT COST •

• AT MARKET RATES •

• ROLLED UP •

• CONVERTED TO A PERCENTAGE •

• LUMP SUM •

Fee Tendering

In addition to the straightforward method of being offered a commission by a client (based on a recommendation or on the existence of a good working relationship), many official bodies/agencies and local authorities look for competitive tenders from consultants.

As a result of this the Landscape Institute produced the *Guide to Procedure for Competitive Tendering*. This document advises landscape consultants and their clients in the commissioning of landscape consultancy by tender. It seeks to ensure that the procedure followed is fair and equitable to all parties, and allows the client to make a valid judgement between tenders received. It provides advice on drawing up a shortlist of suitable practices and guidance on the items to be covered when preparing a tender information and brief to be used when approaching a number of landscape consultancies for competitive fee quotes.

Fee submissions

A standard brief is normally issued to a number of consultants and will usually cover:

Standard brief

- Description of the proposed project.
- Background information.
- Client's requirements: the project.
- Client's requirements: consultant's services.
- Tender procedure: timescale, assessment of tenders and notification.

If a standard brief is not being used, fee submissions will be made in the form of a report containing the following information:

Fee submission

- Examples of similar projects undertaken by the firm.
- CVs of the staff and consultants who may be involved.
- Initial design ideas or outline comments in response to the client's brief.
- A breakdown/outline of the anticipated stages of work, time involved and fees.

Fee calculation

When calculating fees on a competitive basis there are a number of points to take into consideration concerning both the nature of the project and the landscape architect's own organization:

Fee calculation: The project

- Project type (hard/soft landscaping).
- Project location.
- Project value.
- Services required including unusual services.
- Stages of work the landscape architect will be involved in.
- Level of appointment (main or sub-consultant).
- Other consultants required.

Fee calculation: The landscape architect's organization

- Overhead costs.
- Salary costs.
- Profit margin.

Quality Assurance 质量保证

ISO 9000 (formerly BS 5750) is an international quality standard. The requirements cover all the basic management principles of both product-based and service-based organizations. It is a conceptual document that can be tailored to develop the quality standards of any business.

Accreditation is determined by an external assessor/certification body, which will be a member of the National Accreditation Council for Certification Bodies.

A firm whose management system has been successfully assessed by a certification body against the requirements of ISO 9000 is entered on a register, and becomes a Registered Firm of Assessed Capability. Once accreditation is achieved by a business it is a sign of management quality assurance.

Quality management

Quality assurance is about consistent everyday management involving evaluation, monitoring, feedback, developments and correction to assist directors, partners and sole principals in the control of their own business and achievement of their long-term business/management plan objectives.

Quality management refers to systems not products. Good quality management allows the landscape architect to provide expert advice and creative expression, safe in the knowledge that defined systems for all operational areas of business systems are in place to facilitate the project.

Quality manual

This is the firm's own record of the way it works. It should explain how the firm works, the methods it uses and the checking/auditing procedure it uses. It should include:

The office quality plan
Sets down both overall policies and detailed matters such as the firm's maintenance of information services, staff training, resources, identification and control etc.

The project/job quality plan
Sets down the preferred method of running projects and covers all types of jobs relevant to the disciplines of the company/business e.g. environmental assessment; planning; landscape architecture and architecture.

Quality policy
Covers the overall long-term intentions and direction of an organization regarding quality of service.

Auditing
Internal audits as well as third party assessments using the criteria of ISO 9000 against the office quality manual enable a firm to assess whether its business plan objectives are being achieved.

Why become quality assured?

Possible Benefits

Enhanced credibility
- An internationally recognized benchmark reassures clients and places landscape architects on the same level as other disciplines.

Improved efficiency and consistency
- Good management practices reduce unproductive time, which means greater gains in revenue.

Wider marketing opportunities
- Many client bodies are making certification a prerequisite when drawing up tender lists. The number and type of clients may increase.

Reduction in claims
- A well-managed office is less likely to experience claims, and in the event of a claim will have a clear record of the event.

Feedback
- Auditing ensures that lessons are learnt for the benefit of future work.

2   Liability and the Law

The Importance of the Law

Ignorance of the law is no excuse! Everyone who offers a service to others and claims expertise in that service, such as professional people, have a duty to have a sound working knowledge of the law in every aspect of the services they give.

English Law

English law and Scots law differ. English law can be divided into two main parts – unwritten and written, namely common law and enacted law.

> **Common Law – The Unwritten Law**
> - Common law includes the early customary laws assembled and formulated by judges. It means all other than enacted or written law.
> - Rules derived solely from custom and precedent are rules of common law. It is the unwritten law of the land because there is no official codification of it. (Reproduced from *Architect's Legal Handbook* 6 edn, Speaight, A. and Stone, G. (1997). Architectural Press)

> **Legislation – The Written or Enacted Law**
> - Legislation comprises the statutes, Acts and edicts of the sovereign and her advisers.
> - Legislation by Acts of Parliament takes precedence over all other sources of law and is absolutely binding while it remains in the statute books. (Reproduced from *Architect's Legal Handbook* 6 edn, Speaight, A. and Stone, G. (1997). Architectural Press)

Branches of English law with the greatest general effect are civil and criminal law. In addition, European law is now of great significance as it takes precedence over domestic law where the two conflict.

> **Civil Law**
> - Civil law is related to the rights, duties and obligations of individual members of the community to each other, and it embraces all the law to do with family, property, contract, commerce, partnerships, insurance, copyright and the law of torts.
> - Civil law determines the liabilities that exist between parties. The sanctions of civil law are not punishments but rather remedies. (Reproduced from *Architect's Legal Handbook* 6 edn, Speaight, A. and Stone, G. (1997). Architectural Press)

> **Criminal Law**
> - Criminal law sets out limitations on people's behaviour. It deals with wrongful acts harmful to the community and punishable by the State.
> - A criminal legal action is between the State and an individual. (Reproduced from *Architect's Legal Handbook* 6 edn, Speaight, A. and Stone, G. (1997). Architectural Press)

European Community Law

The law of the European Community is enacted under the European Communities Act 1972, and provides that all directly applicable provisions of the treaties establishing the European Communities become part of English law, and also all existing and future community secondary legislation.

Most main decisions are taken in the form of 'directives', 'regulations' and 'decisions', which require member states to achieve stated results but leave it to the member state to choose the form and method of implementation. Today there is an ever-growing corpus of EC decisions incorporated into UK law. The European Communities Act 1972 is the source legislation for all of our new directives.

> - Environmental assessment.
> - Construction design and management.
> - Set-aside regulations.
> - White-collar CCT.

Scots Law

The Treaty of Union in 1707 preserved Scottish law and courts. As a result Scots law is in many respects entirely different from English law, such as the law of property, constitutional and administrative law and criminal law.

The Law of Contract

Two of the biggest areas of civil law are contract and tort. For the law of contract to be of use a contract must be in existence.

> **What is a contract?**
> - A contract is an agreement between individuals, which can be enforced by law.
> - It is the legal relationship between the parties and if it is breached the law gives remedy.

Landscape architects are not party to construction contracts, having more direct contractual obligations such as contracts for services to clients (employers), partnership agreements and contracts of employment (between employers and employees).

For a contract to come into force and be valid there are a number of essential ingredients that require to be in place:

> **ESSENTIALS OF A VALID CONTRACT**
> - INTENTION TO CREATE LEGAL RELATIONS -
> - CONSIDERATION -
> - AGREEMENT -
> (Offer and Acceptance)
> - CAPACITY TO CONTRACT -
> - CONSENT -
> - LEGALITY OF OBJECT -
> - NECESSARY FORMALITY -

Intention to Create Legal Relations

The parties must intend their promises to be legally binding. A moral obligation is not enough.

Consideration (Not applicable in Scotland)

To bind the parties there must be some 'consideration' involved. This means that something must be paid or exchanged for the contract to be binding and enforceable in law, such as money or a service.

Agreement

For an agreement to occur there must have been an offer and an acceptance.

Offer

An offer is a promise made by the offerer to be bound by a contract if the offeree accepts the terms of the offer. The offer matures into a contract when it is accepted by the other party.

Acceptance

The acceptance must be unequivocal and unqualified and it must be a complete acceptance of every term of the offer. (Reproduced from *Architect's Legal Handbook* 6 edn, Speaight, A. and Stone, G. (1997). Architectural Press)

Offers are not indefinite. If a time for acceptance is stipulated then the offer must be accepted within that time. If no time is stipulated, the offer remains open for acceptance within a 'reasonable' time – except in the case of death, bankruptcy or insanity.

Capacity to Contract

The parties must have proper capacity to enter into legal relations. This condition offers protection to infants (in law under 18), the mentally disordered, persons under the influence of drink/drugs against committing themselves to binding agreements.

Consent

Consent to the agreement must be genuine and freely given. It must not be obtained by fraud, misrepresentation of fact, or under duress.

Legality of Object

The object of the contract must not be for any purpose that contravenes the law, such as agreements to commit crimes. If an agreement occurred between two parties to commit a murder and one party failed to perform his obligations by not paying for the crime when it was committed, the courts would not accept an action for breach of contract as the contract was unenforceable in the first place.

Objects

The object of the contract must be possible. For example a contract to build a rocket to the moon in 20 minutes would not be considered a possible object.

Necessary Formality

The necessary formality must be carried out. For example the law sometimes requires that a contract has to be written in order for it to be enforceable e.g. contracts for the sale of land, contracts of carriage – air, land or sea.

How are contracts discharged?

Agreement

- A mutual decision by both parties to bring their relationships to an end.

Performance

- Each party has fulfilled their obligations under the contract.

Breach

- Either because one party fails to perform his part of the agreement or repudiates his liability. The injured party may request damages or treat the contract as discharge.

Frustration

- When performance of the agreement proves to have been impossible after its inception and is therefore a discharged contract e.g. illness or death of one party.

By contractual stipulation

- The parties may expressly stipulate the circumstances that extinguish their obligations e.g. when a contract is entered into for a specified period of time it is discharged at the end of that period.

By lapse of time

- Parties who have contracts of indeterminate duration (employment or partnerships) have a contract at will. Such contracts may be determined by either party by giving reasonable notice. The contract is discharged by the lapse of this time.

Terms of Contract

Terms of a contract establish the extent of the parties' obligations by which they have agreed to be bound. Terms can be express or implied.

The Law of Agency

The term 'agency' implies the relationship that comes into being when one party (the Agent) is employed by another (the Principal) to make legally binding contracts on behalf of his principal with a third party. The extent of authority is governed by the type of agency. 'Special agency' is usual with local authorities where the Agent and Principal contract for one particular commission.

Privity of Contract

The principal feature of contract law is that it defines the rights and obligations of two parties between whom there is a contract. A person who is not party to a contract cannot gain any benefit by suing on it, nor can he suffer any detriment by being sued on it. This is 'privity of contract'.

The law of agency provides the framework within which the application of privity of contract is decided.

Torts ('delict' in Scotland)

Introduction

The law of tort is to do with civil liberty in the absence of contract.

It is concerned with:
- *Infringement* of a *right*
- Resulting in a *loss* recognized by the law
- To which the plaintiff seeks remedy.

A 'plaintiff' is one who commences a suit against another.

For the law of tort to apply, the three elements underlined above must exist in a condition recognized by the law. The 'right' is often a judgement that people have a legally enforceable 'duty of care' to others. A plaintiff would complain that someone had breached his or her duty of care. In general terms tort is concerned with where and how liability can be attached and the reallocation of the burden of losses suffered.

The sorts of situation for which remedy or compensation may or may not be available are never finalized and may change very rapidly depending on current case law.

The law of tort covers many areas and these notes only cover the areas that relate to landscape architects.

What kinds of torts are there?
- Negligence.
- Strict liability.
- Nuisance.
- Trespass.
- Libel.

Negligence

Negligence can be described as the breach of a legal duty to take care, which results in damage to the person or property of a person.

Negligence

Three essential conditions must exist for negligence to be proven:
- A legal duty of care
  You must not injure your neighbour.
- Breach of duty

> Negligence is the omission to do what a reasonable person would do, or
> to do something that a prudent and reasonable person would not do.
> • Damage

Duty of Care

Does the defendant owe a legal duty of care to the plaintiff?

Case law: Donaghue v. Stevenson 1932 The plaintiff found a snail in a bottle of ginger beer, but had no contract with the retailer or the manufacturer and so was forced to sue the manufacturer in tort.

Whether a duty of care exists is ultimately a question of fairness. It involves a weighing up of the relationship of the parties and the nature of the risk to the public. Other common examples of duty of care include that of an employer to employees or one road user to another.

Breach of Duty

Has the duty of care been breached? In deciding whether a particular act breaches the standards of a reasonable person the courts will have to decide two main factors:

(i) The likelihood of injury occurring.

(ii) The seriousness of the injury that is being risked.

Damage

Has damage resulted as a breach of the duty of care? The plaintiff must prove he or she has suffered loss as a result of the defendant's breach of duty of care, that is, damage to property or personal injury.

Economic loss as a result of negligent misstatement is of direct relevance to landscape architects who give professional advice. If no express disclaimer of responsibility is made a person will be liable for the consequences of a statement that he makes in circumstances where he is deemed to have assumed responsibility for the outcome.

Strict Liability: the Rule in Rylands v. Fletcher 1866

> **Strict liability**
>
> Also called the 'Fletcher v. Rylands' rule.
>
> Four essential conditions:
> • An accumulation } together these create a duty of care.
> • A non-natural user
> • An escape from the defendant's land.
> • Damage.

The rule has its origins in the tort of nuisance but has developed into a separate tort of its own. It applies in England and Wales, but has less authority in Scottish law. In Scotland the liability is not strict and fault must be both alleged and proved.

The rule is that a person, who in the course of a non-natural use of his land accumulates on it anything likely to do harm if it escapes, is liable for all the damage that is the natural consequence of its escape. A landscape example could be a refuse tip with noxious discharge.

The combination of an 'accumulation' and the non-natural use are deemed to create a duty of care on the part of the land-user. For a plaintiff to be able to use the rule he must establish that all four essential conditions apply. In recent case law it was established that the accused is not liable if the 'escape' could not reasonably have been foreseen.

Note that this law is relevant to designers under the CDM Regulations. For instance a landscape architect would need to be able to demonstrate that he or she made an assessment of risk during design, construction and maintenance. This assessment would have been recorded in the health and safety plan and file.

Nuisance

Nuisance

Is concerned with protection of
- The environment.
- A person's use of her or his own land.
- Land over which there is a public right of way.

In England and Wales there are two types of nuisance:
- Public nuisance.
- Private nuisance.

In Scotland this distinction is not made.
- Anything noxious, obstructive, unsafe or that makes life uncomfortable may be a 'nuisance'.

Public Nuisance

Nuisance in England and Wales

Public nuisance
- An act or omission that inflicts damage, injury or inconvenience for all members of the public.
- This is criminal law, recently strengthened by the Environmental Protection Act 1990.

Private nuisance
- Unlawful interference with a person's use of her or his own land or enjoyment of some right in connection with it.

Three essential conditions:
- Interference.

- Unreasonable interference.
- Damage.

The activities covered by public nuisance range from operation of rubbish tips, disorganized festivals, oil pollution or emissions of noxious fumes. It is a *crime* to cause such a nuisance and it is not actionable by the public, but is generally dealt with by criminal prosecution. In addition, a civil action may be brought by the Attorney General to obtain an injunction to prevent the nuisance from continuing or reccurring.

However, if a person has suffered some special damage over and above that suffered by members of the public as a whole he is able to bring an action in nuisance to recover that damage (Halsey v. Esso Petroleum). Definition of nuisance has been sharpened by statute in the Environmental Protection Act 1990 (*see Chapter 4*).

Private Nuisance

Private nuisance in England and Wales

Interference may be of two types:
- Physical injury – material damage to property.
- Substantial . . . discomfort to normal modes and habits of living.

It may be agreed that interference has been unreasonable, but courts also consider:
- Community benefit.
- Suitability of locality.
- Temporary nature of the injury.
- Malice.

Damage must actually occur.

Private nuisance may be described as 'unlawful interference with a person's use of his land, or enjoyment of some right over or in connection with it'. The purpose of the tort of nuisance is to preserve a balance between the right of the occupier to use his land as he thinks fit and that of his neighbour not to be interfered with.

There are three essential requirements for an action for nuisance:

1 Interference.
2 The interference must be unreasonable.
3 Damage.

Several factors are taken into account when deciding on the nature of unreasonableness.

- Community benefit. Does the nuisance benefit the community? For example, emergency sirens.
- Suitability of locality. Where substantial interference with enjoyment of the land is alleged, then the suitability of the locality of the defendant's use of the land is relevant. It was established in case law (St Helens Smelting Co. v. Tipping 1865) that if one lives in a town, then one should accept the consequences of trade carried out in that locality.
- Temporary nature of the injury. A temporary interference arising out of a normal user of land will not normally amount to unreasonable interference in the absence of reasonable and proper care. However, if the injury in itself is serious it may be sufficient to establish a nuisance regardless of whether it is only temporary.
- Malice. For example, if a defendant intentionally makes a noise in order to annoy his next door neighbour, it may constitute a nuisance because it has been done deliberately. If an action were committed without malice and totally innocently it would not be classified as a nuisance.

Damage
Causing annoyance is insufficient harm, actual damage must be demonstrated for nuisance to be proved.

Nuisance in Scotland
A distinction between public and private nuisance is not made in Scotland. Anything noxious, obstructive, unsafe or which makes life uncomfortable can be a nuisance. Any affected person may act in the interest of all. The remedy is 'interdict' with or without damages.

In addition local authorities have a duty to seek out and deal with 'statutory nuisances' such as noise. Or a member of the public can complain to the relevant agency, requiring it to use its powers.

Trespass ('interdict' in Scotland)

Trespass
Trespass to land is 'the intentional or negligent entering or remaining on or directly causing any physical matter to come into contact with land in the possession of another.'

Trespass may be committed in three ways:
- Entering upon land.
- Remaining on land.
- Placing or projecting any material object upon land.

> In England and Wales no proof of damage is necessary.
> In Scotland, proof of damage is required.
> *The Scottish equivalent of trespass is 'interdict'.*

In the tort of trespass, 'land' is given a wide meaning and includes not only the surface of the land but also the subsoil and the air space above the land. However, for trespass to occur, interference with the land must be 'direct' and not 'indirect'. Case law (Esso Petroleum v. Southport Corporation 1956) established that the discharge of oil from a ship that was carried on to the plaintiff's foreshore did not amount to trespass because the interference was consequential and not direct. For the same reason in Lemmon v. Webb (1895) the House of Lords held that the growth of overhanging branches from a neighbour's tree did not amount to trespass.

It is no defence that the trespasser intended no harm or did not know that he was trespassing as an occupier's rights should not be violated.

A trespass is only a civil wrong, but it may become a crime if damage also occurs.

Defamation/Libel

Defamation or libel is the publication of a false statement that tends to injure the reputation of another. It must be published and it must be written to a third party. Slander is a verbal false statement and applies in England and Wales only.

Delict

The law of 'delict' is the Scottish equivalent of the law of tort. It is that part of law that deals with the righting of legal wrongs in the civil court (as opposed to the criminal court). The reasoning is slightly different, with Scottish delict concentrating more on general theory and less on specific wrongs. Most actions based in delict arise out of negligence.

Liability

Introduction

> What are a landscape architect's legal responsibilities (or liabilities)?
> * Professional liability.
> * Liability in tort.
> * Liability in contract.
> * Liability as a member of a practice.
> * Liability as an officer in a public authority.

- Vicarious liability.
- Statutory liabilities.

'Liability' refers to the obligation to pay damages when things go wrong. As indicated in the box, there are several types of liability that may concern the landscape architect.

Three of these, liability in tort, strict liability and breach of contract relate to the sections on English and European Community Law above, but in addition landscape architects need to be aware of professional, employer's, occupier's and vicarious liability, liability as a member of a practice and statutory liability.

It is possible that a landscape architect could be simultaneously liable both in tort and contract (and indeed other forms of liability) for a single offence. For example, incompetent design could be in breach of contract and constitute negligence (*subsequent defects*) and, say, implicate the practice as a whole (*partnerships and companies*).

Liability in the Tort of Negligence

The fundamental principle of the law of tort is that 'you owe a duty to all persons you can reasonably foresee would be directly or closely affected by your actions, for it is assumed that you ought reasonably to have them in mind when you commit your acts'.

Professional designers including landscape architects have a specific and wider responsibility and duty of care than the general case in the paragraph above (or than in contract) and that is to all those who will use that which he or she designs, though this may include others than the client.

Specific aspects of the landscape architect's activity may give rise to liability claims if not carried out with reasonable care (failure to perform):

- Liability if his negligence causes foreseeable personal injury to any foreseeable victim e.g. where he orders something to be done that is dangerous and causes injury. Note that the landscape architect is not liable if he orders something to be done that is dangerous only if done in the wrong way (e.g., on the contractor's mistaken direction).
- Liability to subsequent purchasers for defects in the building works arising out of faulty design or inspection of construction works, but only if the defect could not have been known about at the time of purchase.
- Liability to the builder for economic loss that is the direct result of the professional's advice.

Professional Liability

Both the law of contract and the tort of negligence require the professional to exercise 'reasonable care'. What is the meaning of 'reasonable care'?

> **The meaning of reasonable care**
>
> For ordinary citizens the standard of care is that of a 'reasonable man'.
>
> For professionals, the standard of care is that of a skilled man exercising and claiming to have that special skill.
>
> For landscape architects, this is restated in the *Landscape Consultant's Appointment*. 'The landscape architect will use reasonable skill, care and diligence in accordance with the normal standards of the profession'.

The liability of the professional landscape architect in contract and negligence is described more fully below.

Liability for Breach of Contract

For this to apply there must be a contractual relationship with another party.

> **Liability in breach of contract**
>
> A party without lawful excuse, refuses or fails to perform, performs defectively or incapacitates himself or herself from performing the contract.

When a landscape architect enters an agreement with a client, he or she makes a commitment to exercise professional skills competently and with care for the client's interests. So if the landscape architect neglects to do what he or she undertook to do, or bungles it, she or he commits a breach of contract, which makes her or him liable to the person who engaged her or him.

Specifically, duties in contract are of two kinds: duties of care and strict duties (duties of result). A duty of care is a duty to make reasonable efforts to produce the desired result. A strict duty (or duty of result) is a guarantee that the desired result will be produced, making the person who promises liable even if the failure to produce it cannot be shown to be his or her fault.

Usually a landscape architect's duties are duties of care, but liability may be strict either when he delegates part of his work to someone else or is brought in to solve a particular problem.

Incompetent design refers to errors or omissions in plans, drawings or specification, also choice of materials, 'build-ability' and 'supervise-ability'.

The landscape architect is required to inspect the works to ensure that the standard is that originally conceived. Reasonable inspection does not mean a 24-hour presence, but it does mean overseeing the principal parts of the works especially if subsequently hidden e.g. drains, foundations. Inadequate inspection would be a failure to do this.

The landscape architect's liability in breach of contract

Specific aspects of a landscape architect's work may give rise to liability claims:

- Negligent survey.
- Incompetent design.
- Inadequate inspection.
- Negligent financial advice.
- Negligent legal advice.
- Negligence in certifying payments.

Negligent financial advice could be for example, on likely building costs. Negligent legal advice would refer to aspects of the law relevant to the business of landscape architecture. Negligence in certifying payments may include over-certifying or issuing certificates for work inadequately done.

Collateral Warranty
A landscape architect may have a contract of appointment with a client. The purpose of a collateral warranty is to bind a third party (usually a developer or financial institution that is backing the client) into a contract where no contract would otherwise exist. Without a warranty the third party would have to establish a claim in tort.

Liability as a Member of a Practice

Partnerships (unlimited)
In addition to all their normal individual liabilities, each partner has added responsibilities as a member of a partnership. The nature of the liability for contract debts and torts (including professional negligence) is defined by the Partnership Act (*see Chapter 1*).

Any partner in a partnership (in England) who makes any admission, representation or action in the course of carrying out the firm's business binds the firm and his fellow partners, unless it is outside his authority to act for the firm in that particular matter. Any torts, where it may be inferred that the partner was acting as a member of the firm, would be considered as being committed by all in the partnership.

Companies

A company is a legal entity bound by the Companies Acts. Directors may be jointly and severally liable for the torts of the company if committed in the course of work. Employees are not personally liable for acts under tort or contract committed in the name of the company unless they are also shareholders. Shareholders' liabilities for debts and torts of a company are limited if the company is limited, but unlimited for an unlimited firm.

Liability in Local Authority

In law the 'corporation' has a legal identity and can be sued.

> Local authorities were originally set up to safeguard public health and safety. Therefore to succeed in a claim against a local authority a claimant must establish imminent danger to health and safety. This may be difficult to prove, therefore the claimant is more likely to sue the individual professional.

Legal actions relating to civil wrongs committed by a 'servant' (officer) can be raised against the officer and the authority. An authority cannot be sued if the officer acted outside the scope of his authority.

The local authority will be held liable for the act of an employee if the act was committed by a 'servant' engaged in the work of the authority and during the course of their employment.

Vicarious Liability

A person is liable for his or her own torts. He or she may also be liable for those of another.

> Vicarious liability arises from the 'master–servant' relationship, that is, the master directs exactly how work should be done.
>
> This is in contrast to the relationship between an employer and an independent contractor, in which the contractor undertakes to perform work or services, but has discretion how that work is done.
>
> The difference is the degree of control that the employer is entitled to exercise over the acts of the employee.

Generally the employer is not liable for the torts of an independent contractor. However, he becomes liable if he interferes and assumes control, because by doing so, the master–servant relationship arises. An employee or servant is always liable for his own torts, and his employer is also jointly and severally liable if the tort is committed in the cause of his employment.

Statutory Liability

This liability refers to duties imposed upon landscape architects and others by Act of Parliament. (*Refer to website.*)

The Statutory Liabilities of Suppliers of Services

Defective Premises Act 1972
'A person taking on work for or in connection with the provision of a dwelling ... owes a duty ... to see that the work which he takes on is done in a workmanlike or, as the case may be, professional manner, with proper materials, and so that ... the dwelling will be fit for habitation when completed.' This does not apply to factories, offices and warehouses.

Supply of Goods and Services Act 1982
This Act (section 13) says that in a contract to supply services (such as those provided by an architect for an employer) there is an implied term that the architect will carry out the service with reasonable skill and care.

Construction (Design and Management) Regulations 1994, SI 1994 No. 3140
These regulations were a reaction to unacceptably high rates of death, injury and ill health associated with all types of project ranging from new works through to subsequent maintenance repairs, refurbishment and demolition. Infringement may be a criminal offence. This is discussed in detail below.

Employer's Liability
This is based on a mixture of rules developed in common law and those set down by Parliament. The basic relationship between employer and employee is defined by the contract of employment. These rights have been brought together into the Employment Protection (Consolidation) Act 1978 amended by the Employment Act 1980 and the Employment Rights Act 1996.

These statutory rights are mostly to do with fairness and are enforced in industrial tribunals, not courts as in the normal way.

Also binding on employers are the Equal Pay Act 1970; National Minimum Wage Act 1998; Race Relations Act 1976; Sex Discrimination Act 1975; Employment Relations Act 1999; Health and Safety at Work Act 1974; Offices, Shops and Railway Premises Act 1963; Employer's Liability (Compulsory Insurance) Act 1969; Disability Discrimination Act 1995; Asylum and Immigration Act 1997; Employment Relations Act 1999; and the European Community Work Directive 2000.

Occupier's Liability
Occupiers (and employers) also have liabilities for health and safety set down under:

Health and Safety at Work Act 1974
The Health and Safety at Work Act 1974 concerns the general responsibility of employers, employees and the self-employed with respect to both each other and third parties. Infringement is a criminal offence. The COSHH Regulations and Control of Pesticides are related issues (*see section on pollution control, Chapter 4*).

Offices, Shops and Railway Premises Act 1963
The Offices, Shops and Railway Premises Act 1963 concerns itself specifically with the obligations of the occupier for health and safety. Infringement is a criminal offence.

Occupier's Liability Act 1954
This imposes a duty of care on occupiers of premises to all those lawfully entering their premises (public liability).

Health and Safety Legislation

Background to the Health and Safety Regulations

The mainstay of health and safety legislation was brought into force in 1974 with the introduction of Health and Safety at Work Act 1974, which remains to this day the foundation of all related legislation. This is a general document and relates not only to employers and employees but to almost anyone for anything.

Health and safety legislation covering construction sites through both general regulations and construction specific regulations is quite substantial but in spite of this the record of death, permanent disability and serious injury in the construction industry is second to none. It was decided a new strategy was needed that put the emphasis on management of risks. In 1992 the European Union's Construction Directive was published, which led to the introduction of the 'six pack':

- Management of Health and Safety at Work Regs 1992 (amended 1999).
- Workplace (Health, Safety and Welfare) Regs 1992 (not construction sites).
- Provision and Use of Work Equipment Regs 1992.
- Personal Protective Equipment at Work Regs 1992.
- Manual Handling Operations Regs 1992.
- Health and Safety (Display Screen Equipment) Regs 1992.

The Construction (Design and Management) Regulations 1994 (CDM Regs)

It is the implementation of the EU's Construction Directive in the UK that has given us the Construction (Design and Management) Regulations 1994. The aim of the CDM Regulations is to promote good management in the construction industry, prompting all parties involved to rethink their approach to health and safety.

The Regulations place specific duties on clients, designers and contractors as well as on the new roles of planning supervisors and principal contractors. Each member of the team is required to contribute to the overall management of health and safety by working and co-operating with the other members to produce a co-ordinated strategy for managing health and safety throughout the execution of work on site and subsequent maintenance, alteration or removal of the structure.

In all there are twenty-four regulations (*Refer to website*).

Application of the Regulations

Regulation 3 defines when the regulations apply but in more simple terms the following can be applied to check if the regulations are applicable to projects. (Reproduced from the CDM Regulations Approved Code of Practice, Government Department, Health and Safety Executive) Regulation 2 defines the various words and terms used throughout the

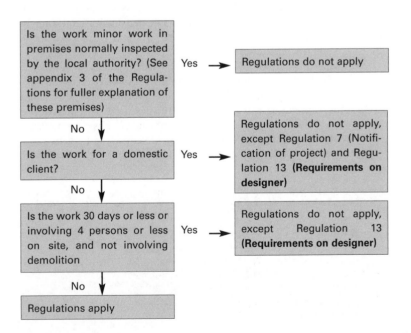

Is the work minor work in premises normally inspected by the local authority? (See appendix 3 of the Regulations for fuller explanation of these premises) — Yes → Regulations do not apply

No ↓

Is the work for a domestic client? — Yes → Regulations do not apply, except Regulation 7 (Notification of project) and Regulation 13 **(Requirements on designer)**

No ↓

Is the work 30 days or less or involving 4 persons or less on site, and not involving demolition — Yes → Regulations do not apply, except Regulation 13 **(Requirements on designer)**

No ↓

Regulations apply

Regulations. Particular attention should be given to the definitions of *construction work, design, designer* and *structure*. The definitions of construction work and structure are fairly all encompassing with the intention probably being to include any situation which is potentially dangerous to employees or the general public.

Duties of the Parties

Each party has specific duties placed on them by the Regulations and these include:

> • DESIGNER •
> • CLIENTS •
> • PLANNING SUPERVISOR •
> • PRINCIPAL CONTRACTORS •
> • CONTRACTORS •

Requirements on Designer (Regulation 13 generally)

HSE have produced an information sheet 'Construction (Design and Management) Regulations 1994: The role of the designer'. At the end of the sheet they state: *'Following the guidance is not compulsory. But if you follow the guidance you will normally be doing enough to comply with the law.'* (Government Department, Health and Safety Executive)

> **Duties of designers**
> - Make clients aware of their duties. (Note: there was a recent prosecution of a designer who did not inform a client of their duties under the Regulations.)
> - Give due regard to health and safety in your design.
> - Provide adequate information about the health and safety risk of the design to those who need it.
> - Co-operate with the planning supervisor and, where appropriate, other designers involved in the project.

Requirements on Clients (Regulations 4, 5, 6, 8, 9, 10, 11 and 12)

As a designer it is your duty to know what these are.

> **Duties of clients**
> - Appoint a planning supervisor.
> - Provide information on health and safety to the planning supervisor.
> - Appoint a principal contractor.
> - Ensure those you appoint are competent and adequately resourced to carry out their health and safety responsibilities.
> - Ensure that a suitable health and safety plan has been prepared by the principal contractor before construction work starts.

> • Ensure the health and safety file given to you at the end of the project is kept available for use.

Requirements on Planning Supervisor (Regulations 14, 15)

It is important to note that the planning supervisor has no specific responsibility for ensuring site safety or that the principal contractor's health and safety plan is followed.

Duties of planning supervisor

- Ensure HSE is notified of the project.
- Ensure co-operation between designers.
- Ensure designers comply with their duties.
- Ensure a pre-tender stage health and safety plan is prepared.
- Advise the client when requested to do so.
- Ensure a health and safety file is prepared.

Requirements on Principal Contractor (Regulations 8, 9, 15–19)

Duties of principal contractor

- Ensure health and safety plan is prepared for construction work and kept up to date.
- Take reasonable steps to ensure co-operation between contractors.
- Ensure compliance with rules if these are made, take reasonable steps to ensure only authorized persons allowed on site and display notification form.
- Provide planning supervisor with information relevant to health and safety file.
- Give directions to contractors where required.
- May make rules in the health and safety plan, which should be in writing.
- So far as reasonably practical provide information to contractors.
- So far as reasonably practical ensure contractors provide training and information to employees.
- Ensure views of people at work are heard and incorporated into health and safety plan where appropriate.
- Ensure when arranging for designers to carry out design they are competent and make adequate provision for health and safety in their design.
- Ensure when arranging for contractors to carry out or manage construction work that they are competent and make adequate provision for health and safety.

Risk Assessments

For every project a risk management plan has to be established, which has to consider methods of *identifying, assessing and minimizing* hazards and methods of *reducing* the loss. We have to accept that there are risks in everything we do but must work to minimize these and take all *reasonable* precautions against foreseeable hazards.

Risk assessments

Hazard: a physical situation with *the potential* for human injury, damage to property, damage to the environment or some combination of these (i.e. the potential to cause harm).

Risk: the *chance*, great or small, that someone will be harmed by a hazard.

The Pre-Tender Health and Safety Plan

The pre-tender health and safety plan is essentially a collection of information about *significant* health and safety risks of the construction project, which the principal contractor will have to manage during the construction phase.

It is important to note the use of 'significant' here, as the intention is not to turn out vast piles of paper covering everyday risks such as the use of cement or pesticides. The purpose is to highlight risks specific to the site, type or method of work that a competent contractor may not be aware of. This information will mainly come from the client and the designers.

The contents of the pre-tender health and safety plan will depend on the nature of the project itself.

Pre-tender health and safety plan: purpose

- Provides a focus at which health and safety considerations of the design are brought together under the control of the planning supervisor.
- Enables prospective principal contractors to be fully aware of the project's health, safety and welfare requirements.
- Provides a template against which the tenders can be measured.

Construction Phase Health and Safety Plan

This is developed by the principal contractor from the pre-tender health and safety plan and should set out the arrangements for securing the health and safety of everyone carrying out the construction work and all others who may be affected by it. It should deal with the arrangements for management of health and safety for the work, monitoring systems for checking the plan is followed and the risks to those at work arising from the work or other work that may be going on in the site.

The Health and Safety File

Information in the file needs to include that which will assist persons carrying out construction/maintenance work on the site at any time after completion of the current project. It amounts to a normal maintenance manual enlarged to alert those who will be responsible for a structure after handover to avoid risks that must be managed when the structure and associated plant is maintained, repaired, renovated or demolished.

The file is a record of information to inform future decisions on the management of health and safety.

Health and safety file

Record of information for future risk management
- As built drawings.
- Service information.
- Construction methods and materials.
- Operating manuals.

CDM Regulations: Breach and Prosecution

In order to ensure that all breaches of the CDM Regulations can confer on the parties the right to civil proceedings, amendments have been produced to the various versions of the standard forms of contract to provide that compliance with the Regulations is a contractual obligation and that failure to comply can therefore also be a breach of contract.

Criminal law
- Failure to comply with HASAW and its associated legislation is regarded as a crime as the acts are criminal law.

Civil law
- Any contractual obligations regarding health and safety are civil law and failure to comply with a contract can only be redressed by an action for breach of contract.
- In addition a party who has suffered loss due to negligence of another may choose to pursue an action under civil law for breach of contract and/or negligence.

Prosecution
- For the same accident on site it is possible for there to be a prosecution under criminal law, for failure to comply with statutory law and a separate action under civil law for breach of contract and/or negligence.

LI Advice Note 02/99: Landscape Construction Work: CDM Regulations 1994 (*Refer to website*)

The Advice Note sets out the LI's current interpretation of the Regulations with regard to landscape construction work. This is based on current advice from the HSE and has not been tested in law.

LI Advice Note 03/99: Landscape Maintenance Work: CDM Regulations 1994 (*Refer to website*)

The Advice Note sets out the LI's current interpretation of the Regulations with regard to landscape maintenance work. This is based on current advice from the HSE and has not been tested in law.

The Management of Health and Safety at Work Regulations 1999 (*Refer to website*)

These Regulations came into force in December 1999 and re-enact the 1992 Regulations in respect of employers' and employees' obligations regarding minimum health and safety requirements in the workplace.

Limitations Act 1980

Loss, damage or injury from landscape works (building or engineering) may not occur for many years after the negligent act that caused them. It is then that a claim may arise. However, there is a statutory limit on the period within which claims may be made.

> **For how long is anyone liable in contract or tort?**
>
> For actions in contract or tort – 6 years, except:
> - Actions 'under seal': 12 years.
> - Actions for personal injury: 3 years from the date at which the cause of action accrued or the date at which the person injured knew that they were injured.
> - Actions for latent damage: 15 years (except personal injury).

Latent damage refers to cases where the damage could not reasonably have been discovered at the time when it actually occurred.

From the exceptions listed above, it is clear that it is important to establish the date at which the cause of action 'accrued', that is, the date on which the cause of legal action occurred.

There is a good deal of case law about limitations and while the summary above describes the basic rules, legal advice or a specialist legal text should be consulted for advice in specific real-life cases.

Civil Liberties Contribution Act 1982

Under the Civil Liberties Contribution Act 1982 a person sued may join in the case further parties and the judge will have to decide the portion of blame attributed to each (Ann's v. Morton LBC 1978).

Allocation of Blame

In cases of tort, even though the judge decides the percentage of blame attached to each of the conjoined defendants, the claimant may look to any one of them for the whole of his loss. If other parties have no resources, one or more of the parties may have to make full contribution even if the adjudication ascribed to them only part of the blame.

Insurances

What types of insurance should a landscape architect be aware of?

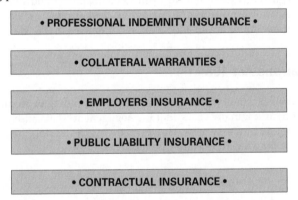

Professional Indemnity Insurance

Why insurance?
The Landscape Institute requires registered practices to take out PII (local authorities also do). This insurance ensures that practices have sufficient funds to meet their financial obligations should an action for negligence be brought against them. It is a Landscape Institute rule that practices have evidence of adequate insurance to be registered with the Institute.

How much insurance?
Premiums are now in excess of 10 per cent of gross fee income. The Landscape Institute used to insist all registered practices had a minimum cover of £250 000 to meet each and every claim with an excess of £500. This is no longer the limit.

What is the premium calculation based on?
- Largest commission in the past five years.
- Projected schemes in detail, including the nature of the work at home and abroad.
- What forms of contract are used (e.g. JCT) and what conditions of engagement.
- Turnover of practice.
- Number of employees.
- Pollution liability.

The larger the organization, the greater the chance of failure, therefore the higher the premium.

How long does it have to be taken out for?

For life and beyond since a landscape architect's colleagues and family can be pursued for settlement of a claim. The practice will continue to indemnify a landscape architect after they have left or retired. If the practice ceases, e.g. retirement of partners or death, PII is paid generally for a maximum of 12–15 years after the completion of the last project with a decreasing scale.

Watch points for PII
- Multidisciplinary practices will have separate insurance policies for each profession. You may wish to consult insurers to check you are covered for the skill required in a job e.g. a small amount of quantity surveying work.
- Give insurers early warning of a crisis. They may instruct you how to proceed. You must obey. If issued with a writ, do not answer it immediately but consult your insurers.
- Additional insurance cover is required in relation to pollution and contaminated land.
- PII will cover the obligations of the designer set by CDM Regulations under civil law for breach of contract or negligence. However, PII companies may require the designer to take out additional insurance to cover the cost of defending a criminal prosecution. (It is not possible to insure against fines or imprisonment for a breach of criminal law.) This prevents designers avoiding set fines by pleading guilty and allowing PII being claimed against.
- If a landscape architect intends to perform the role of planning supervisor then extra insurance is required.

Collateral Warranties

A Collateral Warranty or 'Duty of Care' is a legal agreement that stands alongside the agreement between the client and the landscape architect.

It forms a legal responsibility to the client and funder/tenant/purchaser and can be very onerous. PII companies will now accept standard RIBA forms and ICE forms. There is a standard JCT form for contractors' warranties.

Employer's Insurance

An employer is legally liable for personal injury caused to an employee in the course of his employment by the employer's negligence or that of another member of staff. An employer must provide cover for injuries during employment whether on or off the premises and for injuries overseas if employees are liable to be abroad on business.

Public Liability (third party) Insurance

An owner or lessee of premises or occupier may be legally liable for personal injury or damage to property of third parties caused by his negligence or that of his staff.

Contractual Insurance

This refers to insurance between the employer and landscape contractor for works undertaken as part of a landscape contract.

3 Planning Legislation

Introduction to Planning Legislation in the UK

Town and Country Planning is a means of controlling and guiding the use of all land and buildings in the UK and also the process of change in the environment. It developed from public health and housing policies in the late nineteenth century as a direct response to the increase in population and the growth of towns and hence the increased pressure on the limited amount of land in Britain.

In the UK legislation sets out the basic framework for the operation of the system. The Secretary of State and the government minister for planning/environment for each country fill in the details in the form of orders and regulations.

> • DTLR: DEPARTMENT OF TRANSPORT, LOCAL GOVERNMENT AND THE REGIONS •

> • DEFRA: DEPARTMENT FOR ENVIRONMENT, FOOD AND RURAL AFFAIRS •

> • SCOTTISH EXECUTIVE •

> • NAW: NATIONAL ASSEMBLY FOR WALES •

> • NORTHERN IRELAND DEPARTMENT •

National and regional planning policy sets out the basic objectives of the planning system, and forms the policy framework for the day to day administration of the planning system which is undertaken by local planning authorities.

The Current Planning System and Primary Legislation

The current system of town and country planning originated in the Town and Country Planning Act 1947. This Act introduced the basic system of development control and development plans. It brought all development under control by making it subject to planning permission. In addition development plans had to be prepared for the whole of the country, which outlined the way in which areas were to be developed or preserved.

Development Control
Development control is the term used to define the system for issuing permits for land use development and for taking actions against unauthorized development.

Development Plans
Development plans are the main documents for guiding development control decisions and also for setting out decisions for future development.

Primary legislation is found in Acts of Parliament. Secondary legislation is made under delegated powers given by the primary Act (e.g. section 59 of the Town and Country Planning Act gives the power to make development orders). The primary enactments regulating land use planning are different within each country of the UK.

England and Wales: Primary Legislation
- Town and Country Planning Act 1990.
- Planning (Listed Buildings and Conservation Areas) Act 1990.

Scotland: Primary Legislation
- The Town and Country Planning (Scotland) Act 1997.
- Planning (Listed Buildings and Conservation Areas) (Scotland) Act 1997.

Northern Ireland

The system in Northern Ireland is radically different with the governing legislation being provided by way of Parliamentary Orders in Council, a form of secondary legislation.

- Planning (Northern Ireland) Order 1991.
- Strategic Planning (Northern Ireland) Order 1999.

Development Plans (*See website for Planning Policy Framework in the UK*. Reproduced from *Town and Country Planning in the UK*, Cullingworth, B.J. and Nadin, V., Routledge, 12 ed, 1997.)

The development plan is intended to provide the policy framework within which planning authorities exercise their planning powers. The plan also serves as a guide to landowners, developers and members of the public as to the local planning authorities' main policies and proposals for the future use and development of land in their areas.

The Planning and Compensation Act 1991 shifted the relationship between plans and control to a plan led system. It elevated the status accorded to development plans and secured them a positive role in decisions made by the Secretary of State and local authorities. Planning applications now require to accord with the development plan unless material considerations indicate otherwise: *'there will be a presumption in favour of the development plan'*.

The content of development plans must have regard to regional or strategic guidance; current national policies; resources available; social, economic and environmental considerations; and any proposals affecting the area. The relevant topics to be addressed by the policies include housing; green belts and conservation; the economy; strategic transport; minerals; waste; tourism; and energy generation.

TYPES OF DEVELOPMENT PLAN
- UNITARY DEVELOPMENT PLANS (PARTS 1 AND 2) •
- STRUCTURE PLANS •
- DISTRICT WIDE LOCAL PLANS •
- MINERAL PLANS •
- WASTE PLANS •
- TRANSPORT PLANS •

Unitary Development Plans (UDP): England and Wales

The introduction of a single tier local government in metropolitan areas in England under the Local Government Act 1985, in Wales in 1996 and in other parts of England since 1993 has led to unitary development plans, which replace structure and local plans.

Structure Plans (UDP Part 1)

The structure plan provides a broad planning framework at regional level over a 15-year period. Its purpose is to:

- Provide strategic policy framework for local planning and development control.
- Ensure that the provision for development is realistic and consistent with national and regional policy.
- Secure consistency between local plans for neighbouring areas.
- Provide guidance on the preparation of local plans.

The structure plan consists of a written statement and a key diagram (not on an OS base plan).

District Wide Local Plans (UDP Part 2)

The local plan is the detailed expression of the planning authority policies and proposals for the development and use of land within a particular area over a 10-year period. They:

- Set out detailed policies for the control of development.
- Make specific proposals for the use and development of land.
- Allocate land for specific purposes.

The local plan consists of a proposal map (OS base) and a written statement.

It is now mandatory for all local authorities to prepare UDPs. They are continually reviewed and no longer require Secretary of State approval (Planning and Compensation Act 1991). There is a statutory requirement for consultation with listed consultees including the Secretary of State, adjacent local authorities, Environment Agency, the countryside agencies and also the public. Six weeks are allowed for comment and if there are any objections the local planning authority must hold a public inquiry and allow for modifications and objections to modifications. The local planning authority must publish a notice of Intention to Adopt.

Mineral Plans

The Planning and Compensation Act 1991 excludes mineral and waste policies from local plans. Mineral planning authorities are under a duty to prepare a countywide minerals plan containing detailed proposals in respect of development consisting of the winning and working of minerals or involving deposit of mineral waste.

The plan is to consist of a written statement and a map and in general conforms with a structure plan. Procedures for making a plan are the same as local plans. This mineral plans requirement does not apply in Scotland.

Waste Plans

A waste local plan contains detailed policies in respect of development involving the deposit of refuse or waste material, other than mineral waste. This was previously included in structure plans but the Planning and Compensation Act 1991 requires planning authorities in non-metropolitan areas to prepare a waste plan or include their waste policies in their minerals plan. In formulating their policies the local planning authority must have regard to any 'waste disposal plan' for their area made under the Environmental Protection Act 1990. Procedures for making a plan are the same as local plans.

Transport Plans

Under the Government White Paper 'A New Deal for Transport' local authorities are required to set out their strategies for transport and implement local transport plans (LTPs) under the revised transport PPG 11. These plans will include policies for walking, cycling, bus, rail, motorcycling, seamless journeys, interchanges, timetables, passenger information and taxis. The Government intends to make LTPs statutory.

Responsibility for Development Plans (*Refer to website*)

On 1 April 1996 both the Welsh and Scottish local government systems were wholly reorganized. In England, local government reorganization was piecemeal. The characteristics of the system regarding planning today are:

England	Scotland	Wales	Northern Ireland
Single and 2 Tier	Single (Unitary)	Single (Unitary)	Single Tier
↓	↓	↓	↓
Metropolitan District & London Borough Councils Unitary Authorities County & District Councils	Unitary Councils	Unitary Councils	Planning Service

National and Regional Planning Advice

In order to achieve uniformity in decision making, planning control is heavily influenced by policy guidance. The format of this varies for each country in the UK.

England *(Refer to website: Planning Guidance in England)*

Planning policy is issued by the Department of Transport Local Government and the Regions (DTLR), which has responsibility for planning, building regulations, transport and local regeneration, through the following formats, which are intended to provide concise and practical guidance on planning policies in a clear and accessible form:

Planning Policy Guidance Notes: PPGs
- Explain statutory provisions and provide guidance on policies and the operation of the planning system. They are being used increasingly to set out general policy guidelines and currently cover 24 topics e.g. PPG 3 – Housing.

Mineral Policy Guidance: MPGs
- Provide general guidance on policies relating to mineral planning.

Regional Policy Guidance: RPGs
- Provide general guidance on planning issues affecting a particular region and provide the framework for the preparation of the strategic element of the development plans.

Circulars
- These are still issued but are confined to the provision of advice on legislative changes and procedural matters.

Wales *(Refer to website: Planning Guidance in Wales)*

The new National Assembly for Wales (NAW) provides national planning guidance. The Planning Division of the former Welsh Office was transferred to NAW with all its planning functions following devolution in July 1999 under the Government of Wales Act 1998.

NAW does not have primary legislative powers but can create secondary legislation and develop policy for Wales. It has 11 subject committees and four regional committees to scrutinize current legislation. The Local Government and Environment Committee oversees planning matters and the Planning Division trains local planning authority staff and newly elected NAW members.

Planning Guidance Wales: PG (W)
- The main volume of planning guidance is through PG (W) 'Planning Policy', which is an umbrella document providing guidance on all aspects of planning policy.
- A second volume entitled PG (W) 'Unitary Development Plans' provides guidance to local planning authorities on producing their unitary development plans.

Technical Advice Notes: TANs
- These support PG (W) policy documents and cover 19 detailed topics including Coastal Planning; Housing; Design; Environmental Assessment; and Noise.

Mineral Guidance
- There is no current mineral planning guidance in Wales. MPG 6 1989 applies to England only and is currently being reviewed in Wales. A new set of documents similar to MPG 9 will be produced consolidating previous mineral guidance for Wales.

NAW Circulars
- National guidance is also provided through the medium of circulars. These were formerly issued jointly by the DETR and the Welsh Office.

Scotland *(Refer to website: Planning Guidance in Scotland)*

The new Scottish Parliament was formed following devolution in July 1999 under the Scotland Act 1998. The Scottish Parliament has primary and secondary legislative powers subject to compliance with EC law and section 29 of the 1998 Act relating to 'Reserved Matters' i.e. not acting outwith the competence of Scottish Parliament.

The new Scottish Executive provides national planning guidance and produces NPPGs (National Planning Policy Guidelines) and PANs (Planning Advice Notes).

National Planning Policy Guidelines: NPPGs
- Provide statements of government policies on nationally important land use, planning and related matters. Currently eighteen NPPGs exist covering issues ranging from the planning system and broad areas such as Business and Industry; Natural Heritage and Transport; and Planning, to single topics such as Waste Management; Minerals and Archaeology.

Planning Advice Notes: PANs
- Support NPPGs and identify and disseminate good practice, and provide more specific design advice of a practical nature. There are now twenty-five PANs ranging from Siting and Design of New Housing in the Countryside to Planning for Crime Prevention.

Circulars
- National guidance is also provided through the medium of circulars.

Northern Ireland *(Refer to website: Planning Guidance in Northern Ireland)*

The Northern Ireland Office, Department of Environment (DOENI) works through the Town and Country Planning Service to provide both regional planning guidance and development control. This currently comprises:

> 1 A Policy Document.
> 2 The Planning Strategy for Rural Northern Ireland.
> 3 Planning Policy Statements (PPSs)
>   • Currently six Policy Statements exist, which provide guidance for plan preparation and development control.
> 4 Development Control Advice Notes
>   • Detailed guidance for development control.

Development Control

The Meaning of Development

Current legislation is consolidated into the Town and Country Planning Act 1990, the Planning and Compensation Act 1991 and the Town and Country Planning (Scotland) Act 1997. In Northern Ireland, legislation is based on parliamentary Orders in Council e.g. the Planning (Northern Ireland) Order 1991.

In planning law, particular meaning is given to certain words and a number of definitions are given. In the Acts, permission is required for any development of land.

> **Definition**
> **Development** refers to the carrying out of building operations, engineering operations, mining operations or other operations in, on, over or under land or the making of any material change in the use of any buildings or other land.

> **Definition**
> **Building operations** refer to rebuilding, structural alterations or additions of buildings and other operations normally undertaken by a person carrying on business as a builder. Demolition, reconstruction and certain other similar operations are also included under building operations.

> **Definition**
> **Building** refers to any structure or erection and any part of a building, structure or erection, but does not include plant or machinery comprised in a building, structure or erection.

Under the Town and Country Planning Act (General Permitted Development) Order 1995 and amendments in Orders up to 1999, gates, fences, walls or other means of enclosure are also expressly excluded from the definition of building.

> **Definition**
>
> **Engineering operations** refer to the formation or laying out of means of access to highways and 'means of access'.

Engineering operations include any means of access, public or private for vehicles or foot passengers. Also included is the building of streets, bridges, functional items such as the installation of fuel storage tanks and anything that results in some physical alteration of land, an alteration that has some degree of permanence in relation to the land itself.

> **Definition**
>
> **Mining** refers to the winning and working of minerals in, on, or under land whether by surface or underground working. It includes the removal of material of any description from a:
> - Mineral deposit.
> - Deposit of PFA or furnace ash or clinker.
> - Deposit of iron, steel or other metallic slag.
> - Extraction of mineral deposits from a disused railway embankment.

> **Definition**
>
> **Mineral** refers to:
> - All minerals and substances in or under land of a kind ordinarily worked for removal by underground or surface working.
> - Sand, gravel, top soil, clay, peat, stone and mineral ores.

> **Definition**
>
> **Mineral deposit** refers to any deposit of material remaining after minerals have been extracted from land.

> **Definition**
>
> **Other operations** refer to operations in the context of or in association with building, engineering or mining.

> **Definition**
>
> **Material change of use** refers to activities that are done in, alongside or on the land, but which do not interfere with the actual physical characteristics of the land.

A change of use constitutes development only if it is material from a planning point of view. 'Materialness' is a matter of fact and degree and is assessed according to the following criteria:

- Will the change of use materially alter the character of land or buildings?
- Where an existing use is intensified, does this alter the character of land or buildings?
- If character is only partly affected, is the change material for some other reason? For example, the burden on services is substantial or the change of use has a major affect on the neighbourhood. Or, in contrast, the purpose of the change of use is incidental to the existing use.
- Will the change of use affect only a proportion of the whole site?
- Whether or not 'established use' rights have been lost or abandoned.
- Extinguishment: if a building is destroyed use rights attached to it are also extinguished.
- Abandonment: can it be demonstrated that use has been properly discontinued?
- Change from one Use Class to another.

'Use Classes' refers to a classification of uses of all land into sixteen different types. This was most comprehensively set out in the Town and Country Planning (Use Classes) Order 1987, SI 1987 No. 764 with subsequent amendment and in Scotland under the Town and Country Planning (General Development) (Scotland) Order 1997, SI 1997 No. 3061.

The Use Classes Order is a detailed list of definitions accompanied by subsidiary definitions. For example, there is a basic definition of the expression 'business use' followed by even more refined definitions of 'light industrial building', 'general industrial building' and 'special industrial building'. Words like 'office' and 'shop' are also defined.

Examples of Use Classes:

A1   Shops.
A2   Financial and Professional Services.
A3   Food and Drink.
B1   Business.
B2   General Industrial Use. (Since 1997 this includes special uses.)
B8   Distribution or Storage Centre.
C1   Hotel or Hostels.
C2   Residential Institutions.
C3   Dwelling house.
D1   Non-residential uses, such as medical or health services.
D2   Assembly and Leisure.

Example:

Change of use from bookshop (A1) to a travel agency (A1) will not be development unless the planning authority says it does by Order. But a change of use from a bookshop (A1) to a shop for the sale of hot food may be development because the latter is in class A3.

Not all uses are in a class and these are referred to as *sui generis* (unique). Examples include theatres, sculptors' studios, a students' hostel.

Is Planning Permission Always Necessary?

NO Development before 1947

↓ • Certain activities not considered to be development

• Permitted development

↑ • Other developments including Annex 2 Environmental Assessment

YES • Changes of use that always require consent

↓ • Designated/Bad Neighbour development

• Projects likely to have significant environmental effects

Annex 1 Environmental Assessment

Planning permission is not always necessary. Exempt from permission are most developments that took place before the Town and Country Planning Act 1947 and certain activities 'not considered to be development'. Other activities are deemed to be 'permitted development' and no formal application is usually necessary. These distinctions are explained further below.

However, some developments always require planning permission: these are certain changes of use, designated and Bad Neighbour developments and developments covered by Annex 1 of the Environmental Assessment Regulations.

Between Permitted Development and those proposals always requiring consent is a mass of developments that a planning authority will assess individually on merit. These include proposals covered by Annex 2 of the Environmental Assessment Regulations.

Certain activities are not considered to be development

• Works to the interior of a building or works that do not materially affect its external appearance. Note that putting in windows or doors and works below ground internally may constitute development.
• Maintenance or improvement to highways by the local authority.

- Breaking open of streets for inspection, repair etc., of sewers, cables etc., by local authority or statutory undertaker.
- Use of land, building etc., within the curtilage of a dwelling house for purposes incidental to the enjoyment of a house. This does not include putting up buildings in the first place i.e. a new building does require planning permission.
- Use of land and buildings for forestry or agriculture. New buildings are not included here though they may be 'permitted development'.
- Change of use within a Use Class.
- The formation of hard-standings, except in conservation areas.
- The formation of a means of access to a road that is not a trunk or classified road, except in conservation areas.
- The installation of solar panels and Velux windows on up to 10 per cent of a roof area, except in conservation areas.
- Developments in Enterprise Zones, Simplified Planning Zones and Special Development Orders (New Towns).

Permitted Development

To reduce the burden on planning authorities, the government introduced the concept of developments that are permitted without the necessity of formal application for planning consent. Such development is known as 'permitted development' and is described in the General Permitted Development Order. Permitted development includes the following:

Permitted development

- Limited enlargement or improvement of a dwelling house.
- Forming, laying out and construction of a means of access to a minor road except where this caused a hazard or obstruction.
- Painting the exterior of a building or work other than for purposes of advertisement, announcement or direction.

There are 31 classes of permitted development. Some examples are listed below.

Class I   Development within the curtilage of a dwelling house. This includes summer houses and tool sheds, provided that they meet height, distance and location requirements. These would not be permitted developments in National Parks, Areas of Natural Beauty and conservation areas.

Class II   Gates, fences below 1 m high, adjoining a vehicular highway; less than 2 m high elsewhere.

Class III Change of use within the same Use Class.

Class IV   Temporary buildings and uses.

Class VI   Agricultural buildings and works. (See section below.)

Class VII Forestry buildings and works.

National Parks, Areas of Outstanding Natural Beauty and conservation areas (including SSSIs) have special protection as permitted development rights can be withdrawn in these areas.

1992 Revision to Classes of Permitted Development in Scotland

In Scotland, the principle of Use Classes applies, but the classification differs from England. See the Town and Country Planning (General Development) (Scotland) Order 1992.

Article 4 Direction

In the UK as a whole, permitted development rights can be removed if necessary using an Article 4 Direction expedited by the Secretary of State or the local planning authority. These are usually applied in areas of architectural or historic interest such as conservation areas.

Agricultural Buildings

Under PPG 7, when an agricultural building, substantial extension or alteration, erected under permitted development rights since 1 April 1997, ceases to be in agricultural use within ten years of completion and there is no permission for change of use within three years of cessation (and no outstanding appeal) it must be removed (unless the LPA has agreed otherwise in writing).

Changes of use that always require consent
- Separation of a building into two or more separate dwelling houses.
- Deposit of refuse or waste material on land already used for this purpose that enlarges the surface area or increases the height above the land adjoining the site.
- Display of advertisements on any external part of a building not normally used for that purpose. In this case you need to refer to the Advertising Regulations, Town and Country Planning (Control of Advertisement) Regulations 1992.
- Fish farms.

Designated Development (in Scotland: Bad Neighbour Development)

In Scotland the term 'Bad Neighbour development' has been retained. In England and Wales these are now called 'designated developments'. For these developments formal planning permission is required. In all places advertisement, consultation and consent are required beyond the usual case, i.e. advertisement in the local press. Press advertisements are mandatory and, since 1984, have been placed by the local planning authority.

What are bad neighbours?

- Public conveniences.
- Disposal of refuse or waste, scrap yards, coal yards, winning or working of minerals.
- Construction of buildings or other operations or use of land for retention, treatment or disposal of sewage, trade waste or sludge.
- Construction of buildings to a height exceeding 20 m.
- Slaughter house, knacker's yard, building for killing or plucking poultry.
- Casino, fun fair, bingo hall, theatre, cinema, music hall, dance hall, skating rink, swimming bath, gymnasium (not part of a school, college or university), Turkish or other vapour or foam bath.
- Zoo, breeding or boarding dogs or cats.
- Motor car, motor cycle racing.
- Cemetery.
- Construction of buildings, operations, use of land that will affect residential property with fumes, noise, vibrations etc.; alter the character of an established amenity; bring crowds to a generally quiet area; cause noise and activity between 8 p.m. and 8 a.m. and introduce significant change into a homogeneous area.

Special Development Areas (*Refer to website*)

These are areas not classified as development, subject to less stringent control, or with a special agency set up to promote regeneration.

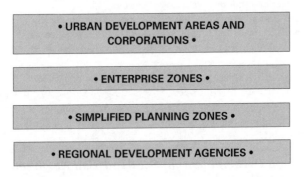

- URBAN DEVELOPMENT AREAS AND CORPORATIONS -

- ENTERPRISE ZONES -

- SIMPLIFIED PLANNING ZONES -

- REGIONAL DEVELOPMENT AGENCIES -

Heritage Planning and Special Forms of Control

Under the Town and Country Planning Act 1990 (England and Wales) and 1997 (Scotland), local authorities are empowered by legislation to preserve and enhance the 'pleasant' features of the town and country by formulating policies relating to landscape conservation and townscape. In addition legislation exists to protect other forms of the UK's heritage.

• TREE PRESERVATION •

• CONSERVATION AREAS •

• LISTED BUILDINGS •

• ANCIENT MONUMENTS AND ARCHAEOLOGICAL AREAS •

• PARKS/GARDENS OF SPECIAL HISTORIC INTEREST •

• LISTED LANDSCAPES •

In Northern Ireland protection of heritage is not covered by specific regulations but is covered under the Planning (Northern Ireland) Order 1991 and Strategic Planning (Northern Ireland) Order 1999 as well as Development Control Advice Notes and Planning Policy Statements.

Designation of Tree Preservation Orders
- Town and Country Planning Act (Tree Preservation Order) Regulations and its amendments (latest 1999).
- Planning and Compensation Act 1991.

Tree Preservation Orders (TPOs)

The Town and Country Planning Act recognizes the importance of trees by requiring planning authorities to make appropriate provision for the planting and preservation of trees. A local authority can preserve any selected trees or woodland through a Tree Preservation Order if it considers that it is in the interests of amenity.

Purpose and Extent of a Tree Preservation Order
- Prevents the felling, mutilation and harming to the health of a tree or woodland covered by an Order.
- Protects selected single or groups of trees and woodlands if their removal would have significant impact on the environment and its enjoyment by the public.

- Prohibits the cutting down, uprooting, topping, lopping, wilful damage or wilful destruction of a tree/trees *unless consent* is obtained from the local authority.
- Secures the replanting of trees the felling of which has been permitted by the local authority.

Exemptions to Orders

Hedges and shrubs, trees on Crown land (without consent of the appropriate government department) and Forestry Authority land (unless no dedication covenant in force and consent is obtained) are specifically exempt from Orders being placed on them. There are exemptions to obtaining consent for carrying out work on protected trees (*Refer to website*).

Procedure for making a Tree Preservation Order

- A TPO must be in the form of the model order contained in the Regulations and it must define the number, species and position of the trees, groups or woodlands to which it relates.
- Copy of the Order, map and grounds for it being made is served to the occupiers of the land and also deposited at a place in the locality where it can be inspected.
- Copy of the Order is served to Conservator of Forests, District Valuer or the Keeper of the Register in Scotland.
- The local authority are advised to inform affected neighbours and provide a site notice if the TPO will affect the interests of the neighbourhood.
- Objections may be made within 28 days to the local authority who makes a decision and stops, modifies or confirms the Order.
- If no objections are made an Order can be confirmed within 42 days but must be within six months or the trees covered will cease to be protected. A TPO can be challenged only by application to the High Court within six weeks of confirmation of an Order.

Penalties for non-compliance with an Order

The maximum penalties associated with an offence against an Order were substantially increased by the Planning and Compensation Act 1991. This major change takes account of the substantial profits, which may accrue, to an offender as a result of the illegal felling or destruction of protected trees.

Penalties

- On summary conviction, to a fine not exceeding £20 000 (magistrates' court).
- On conviction on indictment, to an unlimited fine (Crown Court).

The local authority have powers to enforce the replacement of a tree with a tree replacement notice, which must be served within four years of unauthorized work.

Provisional Tree Preservation Orders

Provisional Tree Preservation Orders have a duration of 6 months and are made when an urgent Order needs to be placed. A normal Tree Preservation Order takes effect when confirmed. In order to prevent tree felling before an Order can come into effect the local authority can make a provisional Tree Preservation Order that includes a provision for the order coming into effect on the date specified.

Effects of planning permission on Tree Preservation Orders

No application under the TPO Regs is required to be made to the planning authority for work to trees covered by a Tree Preservation Order:

'immediately required for the purpose of carrying out development authorised by . . . planning permission granted on an application'.

This does not apply to outline planning consent or permitted development. However, through PPG 1 and attached conditions to the consent the LPA may control what work occurs.

Statutory undertakers' and utility companies' powers in relation to trees (*Refer to website*)

Dangerous trees and case law (*Refer to website*)

Conservation areas

Designation of Conservation Areas

- Town and Country Planning Act 1990 (England and Wales) and Planning (Listed Buildings and Conservation Areas) Act 1990.
- Town and Country Planning Act 1997 (Scotland) and the Town and Country (Listed Buildings and Conservation Areas) Scotland Regulations 1997.
- Town and Country Amenities Act 1974.

It is the duty of the local planning authority to determine which parts of their area should be treated as conservation areas, that is, areas of special architectural or historic interest, the character or appearance of which is desirable to preserve or enhance. Other features may contribute to the appearance of a conservation area such as trees or other buildings.

Once an area has been designated as a conservation area, notice of the fact must be published in the press. Notice must also be entered in the local land charges register.

Effect of a Conservation Area Status

Demolition
- Demolition is prohibited of any building without conservation area consent.

Trees
- Trees already protected by a TPO are subject to normal controls.
- Trees not protected have a special provision that anyone who wishes to cut down, top, lop, uproot, wilfully damage or wilfully destroy any tree in a conservation area must give six weeks' notice of their intention to the local planning authority.
- The authority has then six weeks to prepare a Provisional Tree Preservation Order. If a notice is not submitted then penalties are similar for those contravening a Tree Preservation Order.
- The LPA have powers to enforce the replacement of a tree with a tree replacement notice, which must be served within four years of unauthorized work.
- Exemptions exist including land owned by the LPA and work carried out with the LPA's consent; trees under 75 mm dia.; work in accordance with Forestry Authority licence or covenant.

Advertising
- There are special regulations prescribing the classes of advertisements that may be permitted in conservation areas.

Buildings of Special Architectural or Historic Interest

Designation of Listed Buildings
- Town and Country Planning Act 1990 (England and Wales) and Planning (Listed Buildings and Conservation Areas) Act 1990.
- Town and Country Planning Act 1997 (Scotland) and the Town and Country (Listed Buildings and Conservation Areas) Scotland Regulations 1997.

The Secretary of State is required to compile lists or give approval to lists compiled by other bodies (Historic Buildings and Monuments

Commission (England and Wales)/Historic Scotland) of buildings of special architectural or historic interest.

A building is listed with regard to the contribution that its exterior makes to the architectural or historic interest of a group of buildings and the desirability of preserving any feature fixed to the building or contained within its curtilage.

The local authority is required to give notice of a listing to the owner and occupier of the building, who has no right to object to the listing.

Effects of Listed Building Designation

Demolition or Alteration

- It is an offence to demolish, alter or extend in any manner, which would affect the character as a building of special architectural or historic interest unless listed building consent has been obtained. Application for listed building consent is made to the local planning authority.

Landscape

- Special regard has to be paid not only to the building but its setting also. The local authority must therefore be consulted before making any alteration to landscape within the curtilage of a listed building.

Building Preservation Notice

A local authority may serve a building preservation notice in order to protect a building that has not yet been listed from demolition or where alteration is threatened. Compensation is payable if the Secretary of State within six months decides not to list the building, or no decision is made. The local authority will be liable for compensation, which may include breach of contract payments.

Ancient Monuments

Designation of Ancient Monuments and Archaeological Areas

• Ancient Monuments and Archaeological Areas Act 1979 •

Under the Act the Secretary of State is required to maintain a schedule of monuments of national importance including those in private ownership and those whose ownership is vested in the Secretary of State. The Secretary of State has the power to compulsorily acquire a monument for the purpose of securing its preservation.

Effects of Designation

Demolition or Alteration

- It is an offence to carry out, without consent, any works resulting in the demolition, destruction, damage, alteration or repair of the monument.
- It is an offence to carry out any flooding or tipping operations on the land.

Ancient Monuments (Class Consents) Order 1981

- Covers a range of work for which there is deemed consent.

Scheduled Monument Consent

- Covers other works, which require specific consent from the Secretary of State who is required to hold a public inquiry before determining the application.

Archaeological Areas

Designation of Ancient Monuments and Archaeological Areas

• Ancient Monuments and Archaeological Areas Act 1979 •

The provisions of the Act are designed not to prevent development on archaeological sites but simply to enable archaeological records to be made. Once an area has been designated by the Secretary of State as being of archaeological importance, a developer is required to serve an 'operations notice' on the local authority six weeks prior to the carrying out of any designated operations.

Operations Notice

- Operations that disturb the ground.
- Flooding and tipping operations.

Once the notice has been served, the 'designated investigating authority' (appointed by the Secretary of State) has the right to enter the land to investigate archaeological excavation or to record material of archaeological or historical interest. A notice of intention to excavate must be served on the developer prior to the six-week period ending. The developer must bear the cost of this.

Parks and Gardens of Special Historic Interest – Gardens and Designed Landscapes

English Heritage and Historic Scotland maintain the inventory of historic gardens and designed landscapes. They are statutory consultees for any development affecting landscapes on the list.

The effects of a listing

- There will be a presumption against any development that is likely to have an adverse effect on the integrity, landscape setting or distinctive character of gardens and designed landscapes listed in the inventory.
- Proposals for the restoration of the original landscapes and removal of unsympathetic planting or structures will be viewed favourably.
- New structures and/or landscape works will generally only be acceptable where they will enhance the design and setting of the garden or designed landscape. All works must be well designed, carefully sited and constructed. Future maintenance arrangements must be put in place.
- Development proposals must be shown in the context of the garden or the designed landscape and demonstrate that they recognize their integrity and offer enhancement of the existing situation.
- The LPA will seek to encourage the sensitive management of gardens and designed landscapes.

Planning Consent Procedure

Application for Permission

There are five kinds of planning application and consent. These are defined below.

Definition

Full planning permission refers to an application for full permission with complete details. All reserved matters are decided at this time. Conditions may be imposed.

Before purchasing land or incurring the cost of preparing plans, a developer may wish to know whether or not his proposed development is likely to get development consent if he applies for it. Therefore he applies for outline planning permission.

Definition

Outline planning permission refers to application for consent in principle. Then the local planning authority can alternatively:
- **Grant** outline planning consent subject to a condition of that authority of any 'reserved matters'.
- **Hold** the application for consideration of further particulars i.e. the reserved matters may be relevant at the initial stage.
- **Decline** the application.

'**Reserved matters'** include, for example, details relating to:
- Siting.
- Design.
- External appearance.
- Means of access.
- Landscape for the site.

> **Definition**
> **Approval of reserved matters** refers to resolution and agreement of reserved matters. Once this is approved, the application has full planning permission.

> **Definition**
> **Variation to planning consent** refers to approval agreement of insignificant changes to consent already given.

> **Definition**
> **Notice of intention to develop (NID)** refers to approval of development proposals by local authorities.

Local planning authorities cannot give themselves planning permission, but before the development takes place they have to publish an NID in a local newspaper, describing the scheme concerned and where and when details may be viewed.

Application Requirement

> **Application for planning permission consists of:**
> - Application form.
> - Plan(s) identifying the land concerned and plans to describe the development.
> - Fee.

> **The Application Form requires:**
> - Details about the applicant and his or her agents.
> - Details of the purpose, location, timing and cost of the development.
> - Certification of Neighbour Notification and a list of those notified.

- Certification that the land is not an agricultural holding or that notice has been given to the tenant of the agricultural land to which the application relates.
- Confirmation that the plans are available for viewing for 21 days.

Note that in conservation areas and for designated/Bad Neighbour developments, advertisement in the press may be required.

If interested parties have not been informed, the applicant should explain why not. In this case (and if the local planning authority is seeking development consent) a notice of the proposal should be posted on the land concerned for seven days, one month before the application is made. *(Refer to website for further details of the requirements and process of notification.)*

In **conservation areas**, if the proposed development would alter the conservation area's appearance, the local planning authority publishes a notice in the local paper and displays a notice on the land. Plans will be available for view for 21 days.

Building Regulations

In addition to the application for planning permission Building Standards Regulations may have to be complied with.

Planning Application Fees

Fees may vary according to acreage. Changes of use fees have a standard rate. Other developments' fees relate to the floor space.

If development consists of more than one item, fees may be cumulative. The arithmetic of this is complicated and a practising landscape architect would be advised to check with the relevant planning office for each application.

Local Planning Authority Actions

When a local planning authority receives an application, it must comply with rules set down in the Town and Country Planning Acts.

A local planning authority decision on planning application:

- Must comply with any Secretary of State directive.
- Must have regard to views of other government departments and other authorities.
- Must consider representations and views of interested parties e.g. neighbours and other consultees.

- Must comply with provisions of the development plan (structure or local).
- Does not consider cost or need.

Local planning authority actions

On receipt of an application for development consent, a local planning authority:
- Considers landscape design.
- May call in further information.
- Undertakes consultations.
- Complies with guidelines.
- Considers views of consultees.
- May require environmental assessment.
- May require a bond.
- May require a Planning Obligation/Section 75 Agreement.

The notes that follow refer particularly to legislation and policy guidelines that are relevant to landscape design.

Legislation and Policy Guidelines Relevant to Landscape Design
Under the Town and Country Planning Acts the local planning authority has a duty to preserve trees and enhance the environment by planting them.

In addition, Planning Policy Guidance Note 1 (General Policy and Principles) 1997 included several paragraphs important to landscape architects:

'Applicants for planning permission should demonstrate wherever appropriate that they have considered the wider setting of buildings. New developments should respect but not necessarily mimic the character of their surroundings. Particular weight should be given to the impact of development on existing buildings and the landscape in environmentally sensitive areas such as National Parks, Areas of Outstanding Natural Beauty and Conservation Areas, where the scale of new development and the use of appropriate building materials will often be particularly important . . .

The appearance and treatment of the spaces between and around buildings is also of great importance. Where these form part of an application site, the landscape design – whether hard or soft – will often be of comparable importance to the design of the buildings and should likewise be the subject of consideration, attention and expert advice. The aim should be for any development to result in a "benefit" in environmental and landscape terms'.

For the first time, the process and application of landscape design was recognized and incorporated in government planning guidance. A landscape architect would apprise a client of this policy development and that the planning authority may require attention to this issue, e.g. by the planting of trees.

Circular 11/95 raised the required standard of landscape associated with new development, including design details, earth moving guidelines and enforcement of landscape requirements by planning authorities. Completion of a housing development may be prohibited until the previously agreed planting scheme is complete. Long-term maintenance and management together with more effective tree protection during construction are also discussed.

Other guidance papers include:
- 'Quality in Town and Country', 'Greening the City Initiative'.
- 'Urban Design Initiative'.
- Other PPGs, Mineral Policy Guidance Notes (MPGs) and Regional Policy Guidance Notes (RPGs).
- In Scotland, NPPGs, PANs.
- In Wales, Planning Guidance (Wales) and Technical Advice Notes (TANs) have this function.

Note that a Landscape Institute working group is to write a brief for a new landscape planning policy guidance note, good practice guide or landscape policy guidance note.

Calling in Further Information
Even after plans have been submitted, a local authority may request the applicant to supply further information to enable them to determine the application.

Possible Consultations
Before granting consent, the local planning authority consults relevant authorities.

Consultation
- The district planning authority where relevant (England and Wales).
- Secretary of State/Regional Roads Department for development affecting trunk road or level crossings.
- Highway Authority for formation or alteration of access to highway.
- Coal Authority for erection of building in area worked for coal.
- Secretary of State for development within 3 km of Windsor Castle and parks or within 800 m of any other royal palace or park.

- Water Authority for operations in or on the banks of a stream; refining or storing of mineral oils; refuse or waste; mining; fish farm; sewers; and cemetery.
- Scottish National Heritage, English Heritage, Countryside Council for Wales, ES (all formerly Nature Conservation Council) for areas of special scientific interest.
- Theatres Trust for theatre development.
- Ministry of Agriculture/DAFFS for loss of more than 10 acres of agricultural land, or loss of less than 10 acres of such land if it will lead to losses greater than 10 acres.
- Secretary of State for listed building consent (Category A buildings).
- Environment Agency/Scottish Environment Protection Agency (as waste disposal authority) about development within 250 m of land used, or used in the last 30 years, as a waste or refuse tip.
- In Scotland, the Secretary of State and SNH about development in areas identified in the Inventory of Gardens and Designed Landscapes.
- Secretary of State about a scheduled monument.
- Environment Agency and Scottish Environmental Protection Agency for industrial development.
- British Waterways Board for canals and reservoirs.

Character maps and tranquil zones

'The Character of England' has been a reference (since 1995) that planners in England may consult, produced by the Countryside Agency and English Nature in association with English Heritage. Character mapping in Scotland is currently being co-ordinated by Scottish Natural Heritage.

Character maps summarize a region's historic character, landscape and natural history. England is covered by 159 separate 'character areas' and 22 maritime areas.

Tranquil zones: a technique developed by the Countryside Agency and the Council for the Protection of Rural England (CPRE) to evaluate the degree of noise and visual disturbance in the countryside.

Environmental impact assessment/statement (EIA)

EIA is a technique and process by which information about the anticipated environmental effects of a project are collected, both by a developer and from other sources, and taken into account by a planning authority in forming their judgement on whether or not a development should proceed.

For EIA purposes, projects are of two kinds:

- Annex 1 projects for which EIA is required in every case.
- Annex 2 projects for which EIA is required only if a particular project is judged likely to give rise to significant environmental effects.

(Further detail is given later in the chapter.)

Town and Country Planning (Mineral) Act 1981

A mining company has to apply to the Secretary of State for a licence to work minerals and to the local planning authority for planning consent. The licence is not valid unless planning consent has been granted. In Scotland the provisions of this Act are incorporated in the Town and Country Planning (Scotland) Act 1997.

Owners of any interest in a mineral in the land must also be notified of any application for mineral working.

The Environment Act 1995 revised the requirements for acceptable environmental standards and restoration proposals.

Review of Sites

Every planning authority has to review all sites 'at such interval as they consider fit'. This means that planning conditions on current workings may be updated. This review covers all permissions except where operations ceased more than five years previously i.e. this Act had a retrospective element. With the 1991 Planning and Compensation Act, the Secretary of State became able to prescribe the period within which reviews must be carried out and their contents. Planning authorities may also make revocation, modification or suspension orders as they see fit. Under the Environment Act 1995 reviews should take place every 15 years.

Aftercare Conditions

Note also that aftercare conditions can be imposed as a part of the development consent. Mining will be permitted if restoration conditions require the site to be brought back to agricultural, forestry or amenity use. Conditions may also impose a time limit, up to five years, by which restoration measures must be complete.

Prohibition and Suspension Orders

The Act also makes provision for prohibition (if workings have ceased for more than two years and resumption is unlikely).

If development is temporarily suspended the planning authority may require that steps shall be taken for the protection of the environment. Suspension orders must be reviewed every five years.

Old Workings

The 1991 Planning and Compensation Act includes provision to address problems arising from consents for mining issued between 1992 and

1947. These consents (termed Interim Development Orders) if implemented prior to 1979 remain valid until 2042.

However, planning authorities often had no record of the existence of these consents. They could be reactivated without warning and without the sort of conditions designed to safeguard the environment that would be expected today.

The 1991 Act therefore required these old Interim Development Order permissions to be registered with the local planning authority by 24 July 1992 or they ceased to have effect.

Under the Environment Act 1995 operators of dormant sites must obtain approval for their proposed scheme of operating and restoration before work may resume.

Mineral Planning Guidance Note 13: 'Guidelines for peat provision in England, including the place of alternative materials'

This Note has statutory force under the Environment Act 1995. It describes peat production, reserves, consumption and likely trends in the use of alternatives to peat. It advises that future extraction should be confined to areas already damaged by recent human activities and/or of limited or no nature conservation value.

Mineral Planning Guidance Note 5: 'Stability in surface mineral workings and tips'

A revision of existing guidance is currently being drafted (1999).

Planning Authority Decision Options

On application for planning permission a local authority can:
- Grant unconditional permission (reasons do not have to be given).
- Grant permission with conditions.
- Refuse permission: reasons must be given. These must be precise, specific and relevant.

These decisions are normally taken by the town planning or equivalent committee of the local authority; increasingly decisions are taken by delegated action, that is by the chairman of the committee or chief planning officer, to speed up the process.

A decision should be made within a period of eight weeks unless the applicant agrees in writing to an extension of time. Lack of decision can be treated as a refusal. Grant of planning permission does not come into effect until written notice is given to the applicant.

If the planning authority imposes conditions, these must:

- Be imposed freely, without preconceptions due to previous applications.
- Relate to the application and serve some useful planning purpose e.g. amenity, social need, comfort and convenience of occupants, relate to existing rights.
- Be certain and unambiguous.
- Not be wholly 'unreasonable'.
- Not effect an alteration to general law.
- Be enforceable.

Reason for conditions must be given.

It is a statutory requirement that planning committee decisions pay attention to current national and regional policies, therefore clear and convincing reasons have to be given for any departure from such policy.

The 1990 Planning Act also gave planning authorities the power to revoke or modify a consent, whether full or outline, provided that this order is confirmed by the Secretary of State.

Planning Obligations (Section 106 Agreements) (England and Wales)

The government recognizes that local planning authorities will seek *improvements to development proposals where those improvements would be to the general public benefit*, rather than for the benefit of some specific piece of neighbouring land. Under the Town and Country Planning Act 1971, section 52, these improvements could be achieved by the use of Agreements (also called Covenants). This is a sometimes a controversial and complex procedure that can take many months and is refined in legal agreements.

This measure has been retained in the Town and Country Planning Act 1990, section 106, but renamed 'Planning Obligation' and now called Section 106 Agreement. The purposes for which planning obligations can be used are specified in Circular 16/91 (DOE) 53/91 (Welsh Office).

Planning obligations run with the land and are therefore enforceable against successors in title.

Planning obligations can either require the person giving the undertaking, or successor, to do a specified thing or prevent the use or development of the land in a specified way. Unlike Section 52 Agreements, planning obligations can be modified or discharged by formal application to the local authority with right of appeal to the Secretary of State. The requirements of the local planning authority in an 'obligation' must be reasonable and must relate directly to the planning application itself.

Planning obligations can be entered into between the local planning authority and the landowner or unilaterally by the landowner. The latter are used where negotiations with the local planning authority are unnecessarily protracted or unreasonable.

Scottish Section 75 Agreements
Scottish planning authorities are bound by Section 75 of the 1997 Town and Country Planning (Scotland) Act. The principle described above applies.

Duration of Permissions

Since the 1971 and 1972 Acts all permissions have been of limited duration.

Duration of planning permission

- Full planning permission – five years.
- Outline planning permission three years with two years for details and reserved matters.

Development is deemed to have begun when any of the following has taken place:

- Any work of construction.
- Trench for foundations has been dug/begun.
- Laying mains or pipes.
- Laying out/construction of a road.
- Any material change in land use.

If a trench is dug but no further work occurs, the local planning authority may serve a 'Completion Notice' to take effect within a specified period of not less than 12 months. Notice confirmed by Secretary of State.

Refusal of Application and Appeals

If planning permission is refused, a landscape architect has three options:

- With the client's approval **accept the refusal**.
- **Recommend amendments** to the proposals to suit the local planning authority's conditions, then resubmit within one year free of charge.
- In England and Wales only, **appeal** to the local planning authority's elected members.
- **Appeal** to the Secretary of State.

If aggrieved by the decision of the local planning authority the applicant can appeal within six calendar months to the Secretary of State. Appeals can be made against refusal of planning permission, conditions imposed or the non-determination of a planning application.

The relevant legislation includes Section 78 of the Town and Country Planning Act 1990, the Highways Act 1980, the Highways (Assessment of Environmental Effects) Regulations 1988, the Transport and Works Act 1992 and the Transport and Works (Assessment of Environmental Effects) Regulations 1995. The process differs according to the covering legislation, but the process in general is similar and adversarial.

The normal method of hearing an appeal is by public local inquiry but if parties agree it can be either by informal hearing or written representation.

After an appeal, the only further challenge is by appeal to the High Court on a point of law although judicial review and appeals to the House of Lords are permissible (but rare).

Planning Inquiry Commissions

These are held where usual appeal type, public inquiry, is not best suited to development, e.g. for the third London airport or Sizewell Nuclear Power Station.

Public Inquiries

Public inquiries are not courts of law. Inspectors are usually respected members of the planning profession. (*Refer to website for details of the process.*)

The Decision

Having heard the case for and against, the Secretary of State/Inspector may:
- Sustain or dismiss the appeal.
- Reverse or vary any part of the original decision – whether the appeal relates to that part of the decision or not.
- Deal with the application as if it had been made to him in the first instance.

Technical and Expert Evidence

If you are involved in an inquiry, do not leave preparation until the last moment as the outcome may depend on the quality of evidence.

Evidence should include:
- Any fact that may be disputed by the other side – prove with reason and evidence.
- Any technical questions and answers that may assist the Inspector.
- Any intentions the landowner/developer may have for the land in the future.

Landscape Architect

Involvement as a landscape architect may involve preparation of illustrative material about visual or landscape matters and environmental assessment. After the appeal decision, landscape architects may advise on reasons for refusal or implementation of landscape conditions.

Ethics

As a landscape architect you may be appearing on behalf of either the local authority or the appellant. As a local authority employee you will be expected to defend the decision of your authority, if you are in private practice your client will have appointed you to represent his interests. Either may pose professional and ethical problems.

A professional witness is not meant to be an advocate but to put forward his or her 'bona fide professional opinions'.

Environmental Assessment

Key Legislation

The following comprises the key legislation that covers environmental assessment.

Source Legislation
- The EC Directive 'The Assessment of the Effects of Certain Public and Private Projects on the environment' adopted 27 June 1985.

UK Legislation
Brought the EC Directive into force in the UK through the implementation of:
- Town and Country Planning (Assessment of Environmental Effects) Regulations 1988 (England and Wales) amended 1999 to:
- The Town and Country Planning (Environmental Impact Assessment) (England and Wales) Regulations 1999.

Scotland and Northern Ireland
Due to the different legal and administrative arrangements that apply in Scotland and Northern Ireland separate provision for EIA is made under:
- The Environmental Impact Assessment (Scotland) Regulations 1999.
- The Planning (Environmental Impact Assessment) Regulations (Northern Ireland) 1999.

The Need for Environmental Assessment

Government guidelines to environmental assessment procedures stress that environmental assessment is a process:

Environmental Impact Assessment: A Process

'by which information about the environmental effects of a project is collected, both by the developer and from other sources, and taken into account by the planning authority in forming its judgement on whether the development should go ahead'.

The Regulations require that certain types of projects, which are likely to have significant environmental effects, should not proceed until these effects have been systematically assessed. The Regulations apply to two separate lists of projects. (*Refer to website.*)

• ANNEX/SCHEDULE 1 PROJECTS •
EIA is required in every case

• ANNEX/SCHEDULE 2 PROJECTS •
EIA is required only if the particular project in question is judged likely to give rise to significant environmental effects.

Significance

Significance is a key issue in environmental impact assessment. How is it assessed?

Significance?
- Is the project one of more than local importance in terms of scale?
- Is the project in a sensitive or vulnerable location e.g. a National Park or SSSI?
- Is the project unusually complex with potentially adverse environmental effects?

To help developers and planning authorities judge when a development is likely to have a significant effect on the environment, the government has issued indicative thresholds for some Schedule 2 projects. This is based on a three-tier system of thresholds:

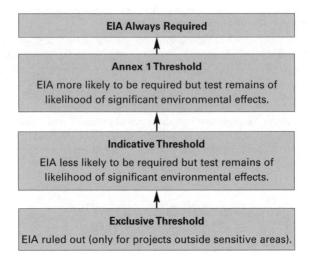

Scoping

The Regulations allow a procedure that enables a developer to apply to the planning authority for an opinion on whether an EIA is needed prior to applying for planning permission. The local planning authority must provide a written statement as to their reasons for an EIA being required. Appeal on a decision is to the Secretary of State who must provide a written statement on his decision within three weeks.

The Environmental Statement

An environmental statement is submitted alongside the planning application for projects requiring an EIA. An environmental statement comprises a document detailing the likely impact on the environment of the proposed development in relation to the information specified in paragraph 2 (referred to as 'the specified information').

Schedule 3 of the Town and Country Planning (Assessment of Environmental Effects) Regulations 1988 specifies information, which an environmental statement has to provide.

Environmental statement and the specified information

- A description of the development proposed, comprising information about the site and the design and size or scale of the development.
- The main alternatives studied and an indication of the main reasons for choosing the development proposed, taking into account the environmental effects (added by 1999 Regs).
- The data necessary to identify and assess the main effects that that development is likely to have on the environment.

- A description of the likely significant effects, direct and indirect, on the environment of the development, explained by reference to its possible impact on human beings; flora; fauna; soil; water; air; climate; the landscape; the interaction between any of the foregoing; material assets; the cultural heritage.
- Where significant adverse effects are identified with respect to any of the foregoing, a description of the measures envisaged in order to avoid, reduce or remedy those effects.
- A summary in non-technical language.

Scope of Environmental Statement

Developers and authorities should discuss the scope of an environmental statement before its preparation. The new Regulations enable the developer to request a formal scoping opinion from the relevant planning authority. The 'specified information' (Schedule 3) covers all potential situations. It is unlikely that all the items will be relevant to any one project and this is why scoping is of particular importance.

Environmental Impact Assessment Submission Procedure

The local planning authority receives a request from a developer for an opinion on the need for an EIA. If an EIA is necessary the developer is notified within three weeks and a reason is provided. For all Schedule 2 developments the local planning authority must determine whether or not an EIA is required and record the decision on the planning register.

EIA submission process

- The developer can request a formal scoping opinion from the local planning authority.
- Local planning authority informs statutory consultees (*refer to website*) listed in the Regulations and they are required to provide any information to the developer as required.
- Specialist team assembled and statutory and relevant consultees are consulted.
- Environmental statement is prepared and submitted alongside planning application.
- Applicant publishes notice in press, posts site notice and information on where environmental statement can be inspected for 21 days.

Environmental Impact Assessment Decision Process

EIA
• ES placed on planning register and copies sent to Secretary of State.
• Local planning authority consults statutory consultees who have 14 days to comment.
• Local planning authority considers representations from third parties and statutory consultees and gives decision. It must not be made in less than 21 days but must be within 16 weeks.
• When determining an EIA application the LPA or Secretary of State must inform the public of their decision to grant or refuse the application and their main reasons for it (added by 1999 Regs).
• If the local planning authority is also the applicant then certain procedures do not apply e.g. requesting opinion on the need for EA, or the type of application (S1 or S2 etc.).
• Public notice is required to be given of any further information that the applicant or appellant is required to provide unless it is to be provided for the purpose of a local inquiry.

Implementation and Monitoring

The granting of development consent is not the end. The developer, advisers and determining authority all have a responsibility to ensure that all commitments made in the ES are honoured. Implementation is achieved through the enforcement of consent conditions and legal agreements. A financial bond is often used to ensure mitigation measures are completed.

Monitoring is the responsibility of the developer and determining authority. Enforcement action can be carried out to ensure that mitigation measures implemented are effective.

Projects that are not subject to Planning Control (*Refer to website.*)

All require an EIA under separate regulations and these are submitted to the governing agency or authority e.g. Forestry Authority, Highways Agency.

Landscape Assessment

Landscape assessment forms part of the environmental impact assessment procedure. The Institute of Environment Assessment and the Landscape Institute produced 'Guidelines for Landscape and Visual

Assessment' in 1995, which the web text summarizes. This book is currently being revised and the Landscape Institute has produced Advice Note 01/99, which addresses the points being reviewed prior to publication of the book in 2001.

Potential Impacts

A landscape assessment should consider two key types of landscape impacts:

Direct Effects on Landscape

Issues that should be considered:
- Character and history of existing landform.
- Status of landscape in terms of existing designations.
- Nature of potential changes and mitigating options.
- Significance of impacts in terms of value attached to the landscape.

Public Perception of Landscape Change

Issues that should be considered:
- Zones of visual influence of development.
- Visual characteristics of the proposals in relation to the surroundings.
- Identification of those who will perceive the changes (locals and visitors).
- The magnitude and significance of the perceived changes.

The assessment should cover the direct effects, both long and short term, on the landscape and on the perceived value that people attach to the landscape during construction and operation stages.

Assessment Methodology

A combination of two methods can be used.

Landscape Assessment

Landscape assessment should provide a clear description of landscape character to give a picture of the existing situation through:

Landscape Description
- Landform, land cover and landscape elements and their interrelationship.

Landscape Classification
- Categorizing landscape into sections of common character known as landscape units or types and their interrelationships.

Landscape Evaluation
- Evaluation of landscape quality through an assessment of the way the landscape is perceived; includes a summary statement about the landscape's importance.

Visual impact assessment
- The 'zone of visual influence' should be determined. The visual envelope can be defined as the area from which it is possible to see the proposed site subject to intervening obstacles such as landform, vegetation and built form.
- The size of the zone will depend on the size of the development.
- The choice of viewpoints should reflect the interaction of the proposed development and the most important aspects of the landscape. They should incorporate both close and distant views.
- The significance of the development's impact will depend on the extent to which it adversely affects the 'zone of influence'.

Prediction and Significance of Impacts

Impacts can be assessed in terms of changes in landscape character and loss of specific elements. Criteria for evaluation include existing designations, rarity or uniqueness and cultural values.

Significance of impacts will depend on the number of people affected and the importance of the changes to those people.

Mitigation of Impacts

This can be achieved through:
- Avoidance.
- Reduction.
- Remedies or compensation.

Building Acts and Regulations *(Refer to website)*

The current Building Acts and Regulations control the construction and design of buildings. They originate from earlier Victorian and public health Acts and now they lay down the principles necessary to achieve reasonable requirements for public health and safety.

4 Environmental Legislation

Introduction

Legislation is a revealing documentation of the state of our culture, scientific knowledge and attitude to resources at a particular time. The content of each Act of Parliament is usually the result of much lobbying and bargaining between different interest groups and the balance of political power at the time when the law was debated in Parliament.

The previous chapter contained a summary of planning law, but landscape architects need to take cognisance of other aspects of legislation about the environment, including law covering countryside, protected environments and pollution control.

Environmental legislation now includes a great number of Acts of Parliament, statutes and regulations. The approach taken here is a selective one, giving an introduction to the law and the many conservation designations that cover different habitats and approaches to conservation in Britain. The emphasis is on themes that have been of interest to landscape architects in recent times.

A sample of issues that have required the expertise of landscape architects:

Water
- Reservoirs, rivers, canals and mill buildings, estuaries, marinas.

Special areas
- SSSI, Nature Reserve, conservation areas, green belt, valued landscapes e.g. AONB, ESA, valuable wildlife habitats.

Historic buildings
- Old industrial sites, archaeological sites, buried antiques.

Woodlands
- TPOs, large forest trees.

Agriculture
- Grazing animals, grade II agricultural land, farm land.

Recreation
- Walking, cycling, angling, playing fields, access.

Transport
- Highway authority, railway, canal board, new trunk road.

Waste and pollution
- New landfill site, restoration after extraction, open cast quarry.

The Development of Environmental Legislation

While the control of development and land use in urban areas has stemmed from concern for public health and safety, legislation for environmental matters has been based on an interest in managing scarce resources; public amenity and access to the countryside; and the conservation of certain natural habitats.

Relatively recent legislation such as the Town and Country Planning (General Permitted Development) (Scotland) Order 1992 and the Environmental Assessment Regulations has extended the interest of planning authorities and environmental health agencies into the countryside. Even so operations to do with the business of agriculture and forestry are still considered to be permitted development and thus are free from planning control. Much country activity, including wetland drainage, woodland clearance and afforestation is only marginally affected by conservation legislation.

However it should be noted that European Union legislation for the environment continues to be produced with significant impact on European landscapes. This was made clear in the Treaty of Amsterdam of October 1997, which established that:

- Sustainable development will be an explicit European objective.
- Environmental issues are to be integrated into all EU policies including transport, energy and agriculture.

Statutory control in the countryside is conveniently divided into five groups:
- Planning law.
- Management of scarce resources.
- Protection of areas for amenity, landscape quality and natural habitat.

- Access.
- Pollution control.

Planning Law

As described in Chapter 3, the Town and Country Planning Acts provide a comprehensive definition of development and provision for its control throughout Britain.

Elements of planning law with particular relevance to the countryside include:

- Trees.
- Conservation areas.
- Buildings of historical or architectural interest.
- Open cast mining sites.
- Designated or Bad Neighbour developments.
- Areas where permitted development rights have been withdrawn such as National Parks.

In addition, this legislation provides specific control of development in the countryside through development plans, Planning Policy Guidance and specific orders.

Development plans

These give some protection to agricultural land immediately around settlements.

Planning Policy Guidance (PPG)

For instance, PPG 7 gives guidance on Local Agenda 21, village appraisals, sustainability, countryside character maps, best and most versatile land and permitted development rights limited by time.

Residential property in farming areas

Planning departments normally restrict rehabilitation of derelict buildings in rural areas in order to discourage settlement that has little to do with the rural economy.

In addition, there is some control of agricultural development. For example, in 1992 a 400 m 'Cordon Sanitaire' was introduced in agricultural permitted development in order to protect residential property from obnoxious odours. Buildings used for intensive accommodation of livestock within 400 m of residential, hotel or office property require planning permission.

Environmental Impact Assessment (EIA)

Environmental assessment legislation becomes applicable in the countryside where Schedule 1 and significant Schedule 2 projects are proposed. For instance an EIA may be required for forestry, particularly for conserved areas such as National Nature Reserves or SSSI, National Parks, National Scenic Areas, AONB and Environmentally Sensitive Areas. An EIA may also be required in other locations where, due to the proposal's size, location or nature, there are likely to be significant effects on the environment.

Local designations
In addition to the national designations described above, many local authorities have undertaken landscape assessments, habitat surveys, access reviews and the like as a foundation for structure plans, local plans and inter-district habitat and amenity management strategies.

The more widely recognized local planning designations include green belts and Areas of Great Landscape Value. These are discussed below in the context of protection of areas for amenity.

When dealing with a particular area or site, a prudent landscape architect would check with the local authority, region or county for information on such designations as these may materially affect applications for development consent, provision of grants and interagency co-operation.

Management of Scarce Resources

Some natural resources in limited supply and strategic value are subject to special regulation generally by government ministries or specialized statutory bodies. These include agricultural land, forests, water and minerals.

National strategic resources

These resources are managed centrally by the government and its agencies.
• Agriculture.
• Forestry.
• Water.
• Minerals.

Agricultural Land

Agricultural land is a strategic, economic resource fundamental to Britain's food supply, which should be conserved and protected from urban development and other forms of permanent change.

The productive value and output of farm land is managed through:
• Grading of agricultural land.

- Ministerial powers to protect agricultural land.
- Weed Act 1959.
- Set-aside Regulations.
- Planning Policy Guidance.

The Department of Environment, Food and Rural Affairs has various powers to protect the productive value of farm land. Agricultural land is graded according to its productive value. Grades 1 and 2 should be protected from development.

The fertile layer itself is also protected. Under the Agricultural Land (Removal of Surface Soil) Act 1953, unauthorized removal of agricultural topsoil for sale is a form of development treated as a crime.

The productive value of land is protected also by controlling 'notifiable' weeds. The Weed Act 1959 contains powers to prevent the spread of spear or field thistles, curled or broad-leaved docks and ragwort.

Legislation also controls production. These powers include authority under the Agriculture Act 1947 to acquire land in order to restore it to agriculture. In 1988 the Set-aside Regulations were introduced from Europe with the initial purpose of reducing food production and eliminating surpluses. Subsequent additions have added further aims and values, namely conservation of buildings, structures, water courses and semi-natural habitats in the countryside and the restoration of habitat diversity.

Forestry

Forestry Acts 1919, 1967, 1986, 1991.

The Forestry Commission and its Duties

The Forestry Commission was founded under the Forestry Act 1919 as the government's authority on forestry. Since the 1991 Forestry Act it has carried out most of its activity through the Forestry Authority and Forestry Enterprise. The Commission owns large tracts of forest itself, but also operates extensively through agreements with private landowners.

The Forestry Commission is required to:

- Promote the interests of forestry.
- Develop afforestation.
- Oversee production and supply of timber and other forest products in Great Britain.
- Promote, establish and maintain adequate reserves of growing trees.
- Control timber pests and diseases.

It is difficult to measure forest cover accurately, but it is estimated that tree cover in Britain has increased from 5 per cent in 1919 to 11.3 per cent in 2000.

Forest production is managed through controls on felling, allocation of grants, forest plans, Indicative Forest Strategies and Community Forests.

Tree Felling

Since the 1967 Forestry Act, a licence from the Forestry Commission has been required to fell growing trees, but there are many exemptions for tree maintenance, small-scale cropping, health, safety, nuisance and work to trees in gardens and urban areas.

When the Forestry Commission officers assess an application for a felling licence, they will inspect the trees and also consult with the local authority and any other relevant statutory authority. Thus, special permission from the local planning authority is required for felling in conservation areas and trees covered by a TPO. Permission is required from the nature conservancies (SNH, EH, CCW and ES (NI)) in Sites of Special Scientific Interest.

In the interests of good forestry or the amenities of the district the Forestry Commission may impose replanting conditions on the issue of a licence.

There are penalties for felling without a licence and replanting may be required.

Grants

Woodland Grant Scheme (WGS)

The aims of this scheme are:

- To encourage the creation of new forests and woodlands.
- To increase the production of wood, enhance the landscape, provide new wildlife habitats and offer opportunities for sport and recreation.
- To encourage appropriate management.
- To provide jobs and increase the economic potential of rural areas.
- To provide a use of land as an alternative agriculture.

New Native Pine Woods Grants

The objective is to establish new pine woods outside existing pine woods that emulate the native pine wood ecosystem.

- Areas will be eligible if they are within a former natural distribution of Scots pine dominated pine–birch forests and have appropriate site characteristics.
- Relatively high grants are offered.

Forest Plans

Created from 2000 to enable owners to obtain Forestry Commission approval for felling and replanting grants 10 years in advance.

Dedication Schemes
Dedication schemes were closed to new application in 1981. Owners of existing dedicated estates may continue to put forward plans of operations for Forestry Commission approval.

Indicative Forestry Strategies (IFS)
Regional Councils in Scotland have been encouraged to prepare indicative forestry strategies, which should be incorporated into structure plans. An IFS is intended to represent a broad assessment at regional level and an outline basis of the opportunities for new planting, taking account of environmental and other factors. The basic aim of IFS is to encourage the expansion of forestry in an environmentally acceptable way.

Community Forests (England 1988)
The Forestry Commission and the Countryside Agency have provided funding and guidance for the creation of 12 community forests on the outskirts of major cities in England. The aim is to include woodland, farm land, heathland, meadows and lakes with facilities for nature study and outdoor leisure and recreation.

National Forest
This was initiated by the government through the Countryside Agency as part of a government strategy to develop a 'multi-purpose countryside'. A private company (the Forestry Company) has run it since 1995. The National Forest is located between Burton-on-Trent, Tamworth and Leicester and is about 40 km east to west and 10 km north to south. All bids for funding have to comply with the Forestry Authority's Woodland Grant Scheme. Take-up by farmers has been low, but altogether, by 1995, 230 ha. had been planted. Participation by landowners is voluntary.

Other organizations concerned with trees include:
- The Arboricultural Association.
- Countryside Around Town (Scotland).
- International Tree Foundation (Men of the Trees).
- Tree Council.

The Tree Council is a registered charity formed in 1974 to help counteract the problem of diminishing tree cover in the UK. It promotes the improvement of the environment by the planting and conservation of trees and woods in town and country and provides grants for tree planting. Its main campaign is National Tree Week held annually in late November and early December.

Water

> **Three main aims of control:**
> - Fair distribution of limited resources i.e. supply.
> - Preservation of water purity.
> - Flood prevention or other harm from accumulation or poor drainage.
>
> **Water management is also concerned with:**
> - Control of pollution.
> - Conservation and recreation.

EU Water Directive
This is designed to tackle both qualitative and quantitative aspects of water management in order to protect the aquatic environment. Integrated water management plans should be drawn up for each river basin, which would incorporate monitoring, assessments of water needs, setting objectives and public participation. The new Directive replaced earlier water Directives on surface water and sampling methods, fish, shellfish and groundwater.

Responsibility for Water Resources
For conservation and supply of water, sewage, inland navigation, amenity, drainage and fisheries overall responsibility rests with the Department of Environment, Food and Rural Affairs in England and Wales and the Scottish Executive in Scotland.

Water supply: The 1973 Water Act created nine regional water authorities in England; the National Water Development Authority in Wales; and water and sewerage services as a regional function in Scotland. In the 1980s the English Water Authorities became private companies. On 1 April 1996 the regional water services in Scotland were reorganized into three 'public' boards with limited public accountability.

Water agencies: In England and Wales the Environment Agency (EA) has independent jurisdiction over all water companies in England and Wales. It has responsibilities for pollution prevention; water quality; flood defences; licences to abstract water, and discharge effluent; fishing regulation; conservation of aquatic wildlife; water recreation; navigation channels; information about rivers, coastal waters and groundwaters.

The Scottish Environmental Protection Agency (SEPA) has some of the same functions, but with a remit concentrating on pollution control rather than overall water resources management. SEPA has taken over the role of the former River Purification Boards.

In Northern Ireland, the Water Executive is responsible for public water supply and sewerage. From 1 April 1997 it became a non-statutory authority.

Minerals

> Gold, silver, petroleum and natural gas are all Crown property. They may be abstracted under licence.
>
> Other minerals run with land ownership rights and may be extracted with planning permission.
>
> Landscape architects should be aware of the land restoration provisions in various Acts of Parliament.
>
> - Generally: Town and Country Planning (Minerals) Act 1985 and amendments.
> - Coal: Coal Mining Subsidence Act 1957.
> - Salt extraction: Brine Pumping (Compensation for Subsidence) Act 1981.
> - Ironstone operators in Northamptonshire and neighbouring counties: Mineral Working Acts 1951 and 1971.

Guidance for landscape and restoration is given in Mineral Planning Guidelines. A new guide on 'Reducing the effects of surface mineral workings on the water environment' was published by DETR.

Protection of Areas for Amenity, Landscape Quality and Natural Habitat

From 1938 a series of Acts has enabled the identification and protection of certain sites for amenity, landscape quality and natural habitat. Increasingly, human cultural landscape history has also been recognized as worth conserving.

The source legislation and the main features of over 20 designations are described briefly below. See the summary table.

> **Designations for Amenity and Landscape**
> These are characterized by stronger planning controls and some support for site enhancement.
> - Green Belts.
> - Areas of Great Landscape Value (AGLV).
> - National Parks.
> - Areas of Outstanding Natural Beauty (AONB).
> - National Scenic Areas (NSA).
> - Country Parks.
> - Hedgerows.

Designations for Species and Special Habitats

These have been established mainly to prevent destruction of species and habitats rather than for active management.

- Sites of Special Scientific Interest (SSSI).
- Limestone pavements.
- Protected species – their sites generally.
- Badgers and their setts.
- Bat roosts.

Designations about Active Management for Conservation

These have been established to achieve a range, usually in combination, of aims.

- Environmentally Sensitive Areas (ESA).
- World Heritage sites.
- Natura 2000 and Special Areas of Conservation (SAC).
- Special Protection Areas (SPA).
- Nature Reserves.
- Marine Nature Reserves.
- Ramsar sites – wetlands.

Designations for Amenity and Landscape

Green Belt

Green Belt (London and Home Counties) Act 1938; Town and Country Planning Acts (for places throughout Britain outside London).

Green Belts are designated areas immediately around urban areas, created to:

- Protect the amenity of towns.
- Check the unrestricted sprawl of built-up areas and safeguard the surrounding countryside against further encroachment.
- Prevent towns merging into one another.
- Preserve the special character of towns.

The first green belt was established around London. The 1938 Act was used as the prototype to encourage establishment of other green belts as described in Circular 42/50. All other green belts are designated under the Town and Planning legislation.

Green Belts should be several miles wide and sacrosanct from new buildings and alterations of buildings unless for agriculture, sport, cemeteries or institutions standing in extensive grounds.

Development within Green Belts should:

- Safeguard the countryside.
- Assist urban regeneration.
- Maintain the essential characteristics of Green Belts.
- Constitute a special circumstance.
- Lend itself to a rural environment.
- Maintain the visual amenity of the area.

Areas of Great Landscape Value

Town and Country Planning Act 1947 and subsequent consolidating Town and Country Planning Acts for England, Wales and Scotland.

An **Area of Great Landscape Value** (AGLV) is designated as land of particularly high landscape quality, therefore any development that is permitted should be designed to such a standard that it would not be detrimental to the landscape quality of that area.

AGLV status may afford slightly more protection to countryside areas than green belt designation, but local planning officers have a good deal of discretion about how that protection may be defined in the local plan. In a green belt it is permissible to build a house on agricultural land. In AGLVs permitted development and reserved matters may be more strictly controlled. The AGLV 'rules' should comply with PAN 36 'Housing in the Countryside'.

National Parks

National Parks and Access to the Countryside Act 1949; Environment Act 1995; and National Parks (Scotland) Act 2000.

From 1949 to 2000 National Parks legislation applied only to England and Wales. Ten parks were designated. All remain largely in many private hands. The Cairngorms and the Loch Lomond area are expected to be the first two National Parks in Scotland.

National Parks are extensive tracts of country designated for their natural beauty and the opportunities they afforded for open air recreation having regard both to their character and their position in relation to centres of population.

In 1949 the aims of management were:

- To preserve and enhance the natural beauty of the parks.
- To encourage the provision and improvement of facilities within the parks.

In 1995 these aims were significantly extended to include:

- Conservation and enhancement of the natural beauty, wildlife and cultural heritage of the parks.
- Promotion of opportunities for the understanding and enjoyment of the special qualities of those areas by the public.

The governing organization for National Parks has had several names:

1949–1968	National Parks Commission
1968–1990	Countryside Commission
1990 to date	The Countryside Agency

Powers of the Countryside Agency in National Parks

- Action on any proposals for enhancement, preservation or promotion.
- Encouragement of the provision and improvement of facilities for accommodation, refreshments, campsites and parking places.
- It may erect buildings and carry out such work as may appear to be necessary and expedient (only where existing facilities are inadequate or unsatisfactory).

In addition, there are:

- Strict planning controls on development.
- Access arrangements.
- A management plan.
- By-laws.
- Special protection of moor and heath e.g. from ploughing.
- Grants and loans.

Areas of Outstanding Natural Beauty (AONB)

The concept was established in the National Parks and Access to the Countryside Act 1949 and applies to England and Wales.

AONB refers to any area in England and Wales which is not a National Park, but which appears to the Countryside Agency to be of such outstanding natural beauty that it is desirable that the provisions of the Act should also apply.

These areas are protected:

- Like National Parks by restrictions on development that would normally be permitted under the General Development Order.
- By the requirement that the County Council (or equivalent) must be consulted in the formation of development plans.
- Management agreements are encouraged to control farming methods.
- The local authority may make by-laws for its own land in an AONB and appoint wardens.

National Scenic Areas (NSA) *(formerly National Heritage Areas)*

NSAs (and AGLVs) became formally recognized by a circular from the Scottish Development Department (SDD) in 1980 as recommended in the report 'Scotland's Scenic Heritage' 1979. National Heritage (Scotland) Act 1992.

A **National Scenic Area** is an area recommended by Scottish Natural Heritage (SNH) being of the 'outstanding natural heritage of Scotland' and for which 'special protection measures are appropriate'. The natural heritage of Scotland includes flora, fauna, geological and physiographical features and the natural beauty and amenity of Scotland.

The legal consequences of this designation are minor, amounting to an obligation on planning authorities to maintain a list of such designations in their area and to pay special attention to the character of the area in the exercise of their functions. Permitted development rights may be strictly controlled. In this, NSAs are similar to AONBs.

Country Park

The concept was established in the Countryside Act 1968 (England and Wales) and extended to Scotland in the Countryside (Scotland) Act 1981.

Country Park refers to land designated by local authorities on their own or private land as pleasure grounds especially near conurbations.

Councils may acquire land compulsorily for this purpose and provide public amenities on these and common lands. The authorities have special powers to encourage water recreation.

Hedgerows

Environment Act 1995 (Part V) Hedgerow Regulations 1997 (SI 1997 No. 1160). This law applies in England and Wales only. Scotland has only 7 per cent of Britain's hedgerows and this legislation was deemed to be unnecessary in Scotland.

> **'Important' hedgerows** are those of significant historic, wildlife or landscape value.

Generally hedgerows should be in the countryside and over 20 m in length. Landscape visual character is not a criterion for designation, nor do the rules include conservation measures or prevent loss through neglect.

This is linked to Countryside Stewardship where from 1992 grants have been available to landowners for maintaining hedgerows. (*Refer to website for the designation procedure for important hedgerows*)

Designations for Species and Special Habitats

Sites of Special Scientific Interest (SSSI) (ASSI in N Ireland)

National Parks and Access to the Countryside Act 1949; Wildlife and Countryside Act 1981 (main emphasis); Wildlife and Countryside (Amendment) Act 1985; Nature Conservation SOED Circular 13/1991 27 June 1991; Countryside (Scotland) Act 1981; Countryside and Rights of Way Act 2000. This legislation applies throughout the United Kingdom.

> An **SSSI** is defined as 'An area of special interest by reason of its flora, fauna, geological or physiographical interest.' The aim is protection of valuable habitats.

(*Refer to website for the designation procedure for SSSIs.*)

> **Points to note about SSSI designation**
>
> 1. It becomes an offence for an owner or occupier to carry out any potentially damaging operation (PDO) unless written notice has been given to the conservancies and the nature conservancy gives consent.
>   - The operation is by agreement under other Acts (1985 Amendment).
>   - Four months have elapsed from the owner or occupier giving notice (1985 Amendment).
>   - The operation is in accordance with a management agreement.

2. The local planning authority has to consult the conservancies before giving planning permission for any development affecting SSSIs.
3. Emergency operations such as felling a dangerous tree may be a reasonable excuse to carry out a potentially damaging operation which is an emergency. The conservancies must be notified as soon as possible.
4. There is no automatic public right of access.
5. Management agreements may be used but are not automatic.
6. There is no provision for by-laws. If by-laws are needed, designating the site as a Nature Reserve may be more appropriate.

Limestone Pavements

Countryside and Wildlife Act 1981. This law applies throughout the United Kingdom. Countryside and Rights of Way Act 2000 (England and Wales only).

Limestone pavement refers to an area of limestone that lies wholly or partly exposed on the surface of the ground and has been fissured by natural erosion and is of particular interest by reason of its flora, fauna, or geological or physiographical features.

Limestone pavements are identified and designated by the national conservancies. It is an offence to remove limestone without reasonable excuse. Fines are possible up to £20 000. However, granting of planning permission is deemed a reasonable excuse for removal. Limestone pavements are protected in perpetuity and without compensation. There are no exclusions for the benefit of agriculture.

Protection of Species

Wildlife and Countryside Act 1981 amended 1985 (replacing Protection of Birds Acts 1954–1967 and Conservation of Wild Creatures and Wild Plants Act 1975); SOED Circular 13/1991. Also the Convention on International Trade in Endangered Species of Wild Fauna and Flora (CITES) and European Wildlife Trade Regulations (EC 338/97). Wild Mammals (Protection) Act 1996. The scope of the Wildlife and Countryside Act is reviewed every five years, most recently in 1998. The revision of schedules is contained in Statutory Orders 1989–1995. Countryside and Rights of Way Act 2000.

This law applies throughout the United Kingdom. Its purpose is the protection of wildlife, habitats and species. See the diagram on p.112 for a summary of the law. (*Refer to website for details*)

Sites   *Examples*

PROTECTION OF SPECIES

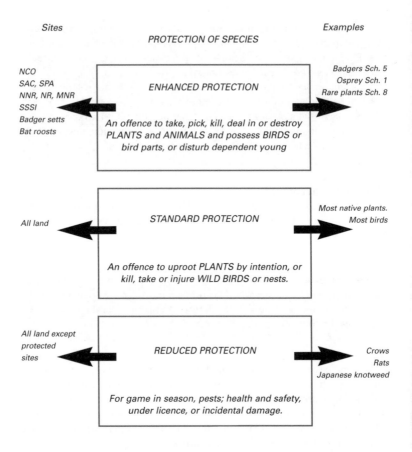

NCO
SAC, SPA
NNR, NR, MNR
SSSI
Badger setts
Bat roosts

ENHANCED PROTECTION

*An offence to take, pick, kill, deal in or destroy
PLANTS and ANIMALS and possess BIRDS or
bird parts, or disturb dependent young*

*Badgers Sch. 5
Osprey Sch. 1
Rare plants Sch. 8*

All land

STANDARD PROTECTION

*An offence to uproot PLANTS by intention, or
kill, take or injure WILD BIRDS or nests.*

*Most native plants.
Most birds*

*All land except
protected
sites*

REDUCED PROTECTION

*For game in season, pests; health and safety,
under licence, or incidental damage.*

*Crows
Rats
Japanese knotweed*

Convention on International Trade in Endangered Species (CITES)

CITES has been strengthened by new European wildlife legislation, which
came into effect from 1 June 1997, that will control or ban the trade of
over 25 000 species of animals, birds and plants (European Wildlife Trade
Regulations EC 338/97).

UK Biodiversity Action Plan (UKBAP)

Following the 1992 UN Convention on Biodiversity, the UK Biodiversity Action Plan was endorsed by the government in May 1996. It includes 116 species action plans and 14 habitat action plans for Britain's most rapidly declining and endangered species and habitats. It includes ambitious targets for recovery e.g. to create 6000 ha. of lowland heath by 2005.

The EU Biodiversity Strategy was adopted in February 1998. The aims of the EU strategy are 'to anticipate, prevent and attack the causes of significant reduction or loss of biological diversity at source'. Objectives are approached through 'sectoral action plans' e.g. for agriculture, fisheries and regional policies.

Badgers and their Setts

Wildlife and Countryside (Amendment) Act 1985; Wildlife and Countryside Act 1981; Badger Act 1973. Protection of Badgers Act 1992. This law applies throughout the United Kingdom.

The killing or taking of **badgers** is prohibited by the Wildlife and Countryside Act 1981. Since 1985 Act, **badger setts** have also been protected. For both killing and injuring badgers or damaging of setts, the normal onus of proof is reversed: an accused must prove his innocence (strict liability).

Badger numbers may be controlled under licence.

Bats and Bat Roosts

Wildlife and Countryside Act 1981. This law applies throughout the United Kingdom.

It is an offence to kill, take or disturb **bats** in the non-living area of a dwelling house or any other place without first notifying the conservancies. The conservancies must be given reasonable time to advise.

Designations about Active Management for Conservation

Environmentally Sensitive Areas (ESA)

Agriculture Act 1986. The Act applies throughout the United Kingdom.

Environmentally Sensitive Areas are farm areas of outstanding ecological or landscape importance that are under threat from actual or potential changes in farming practice.

Aims for ESAs

Designation should encourage the maintenance or adoption of agricultural methods that facilitate British agricultural policy and achieve a balance between four sets of interests, which may conflict:
- The provision and maintenance of a stable agricultural industry.
- The economic and social interest of rural areas.
- The conservation and enhancement of the natural beauty and amenity of the countryside (including its flora and fauna, geological and physiographical features) and any features of archaeological, architectural and historic interest.
- The provision of enjoyment by the public.

The main output of designation is a management agreement between the Secretary of State and those with interest in the land in return for payment. The designation order may specify:

- Agricultural practices/operations to be used, usually traditional methods.
- A minimum period of an agreement.
- Provision for breach of agreement.
- Rate of payment.

Note that ESA agreements are vulnerable when farmers learn that they may realize greater profit by using the land for crops heavily supported by the Common Agricultural Policy than by accepting ESA payment.

In Scotland, no new ESAs were designated from January 2001. A new scheme called Rural Stewardship was introduced instead.

World Heritage Sites

A designation based on the Convention for the Protection of the World Cultural and Natural Heritage 1972.

World Heritage sites are the natural and man-made treasures of the world. Sites have 'outstanding universal value' for science, aesthetics or nature conservation.

The World Heritage Committee of UNESCO identifies sites according to strict criteria. States are expected to take active and utmost steps to conserve these sites and educate the public to appreciate them. International assistance may be available to promote their recognition and protection.

Examples in Britain include St Kilda, Stonehenge, Ironbridge and Edinburgh New Town. Examples abroad include the Grand Canyon and the Taj Mahal.

The Habitats Directive 'Natura 2000' (SAC)

Conservation of natural habitats and wild flora and fauna – Directive 92/43 (OJL206, 22 July 1992). This is an extension to the Birds Directive 79/409 and like the Birds Directive is a consequence of the Bern Convention of European Wildlife and Natural Habitats 1979. The Directive is implemented in the UK under the Conservation (Natural Habitats etc.) Regulations 1994 (1995 in N. Ireland) and enabled by the European Communities Act 1972.

> **Natura 2000** refers to a network of important sites for birds, plants and mammals. The bird sites are designated as **Special Protection Areas (SPAs)**. Sites for plants and animals are designated as **Special Areas of Conservation (SACs)**. SACs are terrestrial or marine areas that support rare, endangered or vulnerable natural habitats and species of plants or animals (other than birds). They will require protection and positive management in the interests of the habitats or species for which they are established.

This is an important conservation measure, intended to maintain biodiversity in the Community and to maintain or restore 'favourable conservation status' for habitats and wild species of flora and fauna identified as being of Community interest.

Environment assessment is a key part of the Directive. Projects may go ahead only if they do not damage the integrity of the site. However, if the project or plan must go ahead 'for imperative reasons of a social or economic nature' the authorities must take compensating measures to preserve Natura 2000 network.

UK government policy is that all Natura 2000 sites must first be designated SSSIs (or Areas of Special Scientific Interest – ASSIs in N. Ireland). The schedule of Potentially Damaging Operations associated with SSSIs can be reviewed and amended with immediate effect if proposed operations are incompatible with the conservation objectives of the Natura 2000 site.

Special Protection Areas

> **Special Protection Areas for birds (SPA)**
>
> This designation was required by EC Birds Directive 79/409 and amendments. It provides Community-wide protection for all wild birds and their habitats. SPAs are selected on the basis that the site and its habitat support alternatively:
> - 20 000 waterfowl or seabirds.
> - 1 per cent of the GB population of birds listed in Annex I of the Birds Directive.
> - 1 per cent of the biogeographical population of a migratory species.
>
> Once designated, member states must take 'appropriate steps to avoid pollution or deterioration of habitats or any disturbances affecting the birds'.

Nature Reserves

National Parks and Access to the Countryside Act 1949, reinforced by the Wildlife and Countryside Act 1981. This law applies to England, Wales and Scotland.

> A **Nature Reserve** is designated land managed for the study, research or preservation of flora, fauna, geology or physiographical features.

Opportunities for education are required for designation to be approved.

Nature Reserve status provides significant protection for land and habitats through by-laws and other rules. For example, orders may be made restricting or prohibiting vehicles on roads in a reserve in England or Wales. Also the conservancies must be consulted before road building or improvement in or near a reserve is initiated. Reserve land cannot be included in Farm Woodland Premium Schemes.

Parties Involved

Nature Reserves may be set up and managed by the nature conservancies or by local authorities or the two jointly. They enter an agreement with the occupier, lessee or an owner to establish a Nature Reserve. Costs are borne by the conservancy, the owners or jointly.

By-laws

The conservancies can make by-laws for protection of the site as long as they do not interfere with owner's rights or with a public right of way, statutory undertakers, drainage authorities, salmon fishery, district boards or telecommunications bodies.

Dedication, Covenant or Management Agreement

These run with the land and identify any special management requirements for the site. Management agreements may stipulate works to be undertaken, payment for works and compensation for the loss of parties' rights.

Compulsory Acquisition

The conservancies may acquire a site compulsorily if they believe the site would be managed as a nature reserve, say by the RSPB, or if the management agreement has not been reached on reasonable terms or has been broken and notice sent to the owner.

National Nature Reserves

If it is of sufficient importance, the nature conservancy may designate a site as a National Nature Reserve and manage it itself or by an approved body such as the RSPB. Such a site would normally be made an SSSI, but also have by-laws for greater statutory protection.

Marine Nature Reserves

Marine Nature Reserves are designated under the Wildlife and Countryside Act 1981. The law applies throughout the United Kingdom.

Marine Nature Reserves

To conserve marine flora or fauna or geological or physiographical features of special interest, or for suitable conditions for the study and research of those interested in any area of sea or tidal water and the land so covered. The reserve may extend from the seaward limit of territorial water to the high water mark and include tidal parts of rivers and estuaries.

The conservancies manage the sites and may make by-laws to restrict entry of persons or vessels, prohibit acts damaging to animals, plants and fish and the deposit of rubbish.

However, by-laws cannot restrict non-pleasure boats, or even exclude such boats at all times of year. Actions to safeguard a vessel or life cannot be rendered unlawful by by-laws; nor can discharge from a vessel; or activity more than 30 m below the seabed. By-laws cannot restrict activity of local authorities, the Environment Agency, water or sewerage authorities, SEPA, navigation, harbour, pilotage and lighthouse authorities, salmon fishery district boards and local fishery committees. In short, protection of these reserves is weak.

Integrated Coastal Zone Management (ICZM)

An EU demonstration programme initiated in 1997 to run for three years, intended to investigate existing pressures on the environment in coastal areas; current action for environmental management; development and planning; and causes of current problems. ICZM is not yet supported by legislation.

Convention of Wetlands of International Importance (Ramsar sites)

Ramsar sites are of national significance for ecology, botany, zoology, limnology or hydrology. Sites regularly supporting 10 000 ducks or geese or 1 per cent of the breeding pair population of a species should be designated and protected.

This agreement is also known as the Ramsar Convention after the town in Iran where the convention was signed in 1971. The Convention makes provisions for the protection of wetlands throughout the world, which are disappearing as a result of drainage, land reclamation and pollution.

Ramsar sites are now covered by legislation in the Countryside and Rights of Way Act 2000 (England and Wales only) but as a matter of policy the government has chosen to apply the same consideration to the protection of Ramsar sites as is given to Special Protection Areas (SPAs). The list of sites is maintained by the International Union for the Conservation of Nature (IUCN), which must be apprised of any changes in site.

Means of protection or management
- Management agreements.
- Nature Conservation Order.
- Special Nature Conservation Order.
- Sanctuary Order.

Management Agreements

National Parks and Access to the Countryside Act 1949; Countryside Act 1968; Wildlife and Countryside Act 1981; Countryside (Scotland) Act 1981.

A **management agreement** is an agreement for the conservation or enhancement of the natural beauty or amenity of land in the countryside or the promotion of public enjoyment of such land.

A management agreement is a deed binding both parties. It contains undertakings by both parties, which are called covenants. Breach of covenant by one party enables the other to bring an action for damages or for an injunction to restrain that breach. The agreement is made between a local planning authority or conservancy and any person with an interest in land, e.g. the owner or tenant. The agreement runs with the land entered into by owner or tenant for life.

Management agreements may contain:
- Restrictions on certain methods of cultivation or change of use.
- Restrictions on the exercise of rights over land e.g. no shooting.
- Obligation on the owner/occupier to carry out certain works.
- Permission for the Local Planning Authority to carry out works to fulfil their functions under the National Parks etc. Act 1949 or the Countryside Act 1968 e.g. picnic sites.
- Financial payments.

Management agreements may be used in National Parks, SSSIs, National Nature Reserves, Nature Conservation Orders, ESAs, Countryside Stewardship, and the Natura 2000 SAC network.

Sanctuary Order

Sanctuary Order refers to an order made by the Secretary of State to protect wild birds or specified birds, nests, eggs, or dependent young at any time or for a specified period. The Order can make it an offence for any unauthorized person to enter such an area of special protection.

Nature Conservation Order (NCO)

Wildlife and Countryside Act 1981. This law applies in Scotland, England and Wales.

A **Nature Conservation Order** refers to an instruction that land is of special interest for its flora, fauna, and geological or physiographical interest and shall be designated by an NCO:
- To ensure the survival in Great Britain of any kind of animal or plant.
- To comply with an international obligation.
- Where land is of national importance, to ensure its natural features of interest.

Characteristics of an NCO
- NCOs come into effect immediately, therefore they are used for urgent protection, usually used in conjunction with SSSIs.
- Potentially damaging operations have to be specified. It is an offence for the owner, occupier or any other person (only owners or occupiers are liable in SSSIs) to carry out the specified operation unless written notice is given to the conservancies and:
    - The conservancies give consent.
    - The work is in accordance with a management agreement.
    - Three months have elapsed from the notice of intention. This period can be extended (unlike in SSSIs).
- No offence is committed if work in emergency or with planning permission.
- If a prohibited operation is carried out unlawfully, the offender can be prosecuted and obliged to restore the land to its previous condition.
- Compensation may be available to an owner or tenant affected by an NCO.
- NCOs are made on the recommendation of the conservancies. The owner or lessee is informed of the designation and may make representation to the Secretary of State if she or he objects or wishes modifications. The case would be decided by local public inquiry.

Special Nature Conservation Orders

Wildlife and Countryside Act 1981 and Conservation (Natural Habitats etc.) Regulations 1994. This law applies throughout the United Kingdom.

Special Nature Conservation Order refers to a designation authorized by a Secretary of State to protect Natura 2000 sites. It is the most stringent protection possible.

No time limits are specified after which an owner or occupier can carry out a potentially damaging operation (compare with NCO above). A PDO can be carried out only with written consent of a conservancy or in accordance with a management agreement.

Access to the Countryside

Public rights of access in Britain are restricted to specific locations: the Queen's highway, the foreshore, common land and to specific routes described below.

Public Rights of Way in England and Wales

National Park and Access to Countryside Act 1949; Countryside Act 1968; Wildlife and Countryside Act 1981; Highways Act 1980 (sections 25 and 26); Rights of Way Act 1990; Countryside and Rights of Way Act 2000.

> The Countryside Act 1981 defined **three types of route**: footpath, bridleway and byway. A byway is where there are vehicular rights over a route. Routes are recorded on **definitive maps** with a **statement** describing the route. The Countryside and Rights of Way Act 2000 created a fourth type of route, called 'restricted by ways'.

Under the National Park and Access to Countryside Act 1949, county councils had to survey and keep up-to-date records of public footpaths, bridleways and roads used as public footpaths and bridleways.

> **Legal consequences of definitive maps**
> - If the map indicates a public footpath or bridleway or byway, that designation is conclusive evidence that right exists (but does not preclude the possibility that a greater public right may exist).
> - The written statement is conclusive as to the position and width of the appropriate right of way.
> - It is a criminal offence to keep a bull of a dairy herd of cows or heifers at large in a field or enclosure crossed by a public right of way.
> - Occupiers are obliged to restore a footpath or bridleway that crosses a field as soon as possible after ploughing it, and in any case within two weeks. It is an offence to plough footpaths or bridleways along the side or headland of a field. Local authorities are empowered to restore unlawfully ploughed routes.
> - Local authorities are required to erect signs at every point where a public footpath, bridleway or byway leaves a metalled road (unless agreed to be unnecessary). Signs may also be erected along a route by agreement with the landowner or occupier.
> - Copies of maps and statements must be available for public viewing.

New routes can be created in several ways:

- The public can request that a route be added to the map and statement after 20 years of uninterrupted use. If the county council refuses, there is appeal to the Secretary of State.
- Public path agreement – a dedication of the landowner.
- Public path order – compulsory powers used by a local authority.

Before new paths are created or existing ones are stopped up or diverted there must be publicity, objections and representations made and affected owners and occupiers informed. If there are no objections the county council confirms the route. If there are objections there will be a public local inquiry or private hearing.

The Countryside and Rights of Way Act 2000 requires local authorities to complete their records of historic routes. Most public rights of way not recorded on definitive maps by 2026 will be extinguished.

Under the Countryside and Rights of Way Act 2000, (section 60), every local highway authority has to publish a rights of way 'improvement plan' by 2005. The plan would follow assessment of whether or not existing routes meet the current and future needs of the public, opportunities for open-air recreation and access for blind and partially sighted people or others with mobility difficulties.

The Countryside and Rights of Way Act 2000 makes it clear that driving any motor vehicle (including motor bikes, quad bikes and scrambler bikes) on footpaths, bridleways, restricted byways (formerly called Roads Used as Public Paths) or off-road is an offence, unless the driver has lawful authority.

Public Rights of Way in Scotland

Countryside (Scotland) Act 1967.

Duties of Local Authorities
In Scotland, under the 1967 Act, local authorities have a duty to keep public rights of way open. They may facilitate access by installing gates, stiles and signs. They do *not* have a duty to maintain routes, that is the responsibility of the landowner.

Identification of Public Rights of Way
The system of definitive maps and statements used in England and Wales to establish legal authority to public rights of way does not exist in Scotland. To have such legal certainty in Scotland, each route has to be surveyed and tested individually in court. However certain criteria may be used to identify likely public rights of way:

Some criteria to identify public rights of way in Scotland

- Routes must connect two public places to which the public resort for some definite or intelligible purpose.
- Routes must be reasonably well defined and capable of being followed from end to end.
- The route must have been used by the general public openly, peaceably and without judicial interruption for a continuous period of not less than 20 years if the use is for a period ending after 25 July 1976.
- Use of public right of way must be as a matter of right and not merely a matter of tolerance or licence on the part of the proprietor of the land over which the right of way runs.

Access agreement and order

National Parks and Access to the Countryside Act 1949; Countryside (Scotland) Act 1967; Countryside Act 1968. This applies throughout the United Kingdom.

Access agreements and orders are created to enable the public to have access for open-air recreation to open country, consisting wholly or predominantly of mountain, moor, heath, down, cliff or foreshore including banks, barriers, dune, beach, flat or other land adjacent to the foreshore. Also included are rivers and canals, connecting expanses of water and the land adjacent to them which is sufficient for access on foot, using boats and picnicking.

Local authorities may provide for access by acquiring land themselves, by access agreements with landowners or by compulsory access orders.

Consequences

- A landowner is not responsible to the public using such rights of access to the same extent as he would be to other authorized visitors.
- The public become trespassers if they abuse these rights e.g. damage property, light fires, harm wildlife or stock, deposit rubbish, hold political meetings or generally annoy other people.
- Local authorities (in England and Wales) are required to keep maps showing land in their area open for public access. In Scotland local authorities must map areas covered by access agreements.
- Access agreements may include payment incurred in implementing an agreement.
- By-laws can be made and wardens appointed by the local planning authority.

Excepted land
- Agricultural land other than livestock grazing.
- Land covered by buildings or curtilage of such.
- Land plus curtilage for surface mineral extraction, golf courses, sports grounds, racecourses, airfields.
- Land undergoing development for any of the above.

Access orders are made on the authority of local planning authorities and must be confirmed by the Secretary of State. They can be recommended by the conservancies or required by the Secretary of State. The order must include a map defining the land concerned. An order may specify work or other things to be done on the land to facilitate recreational use.

Public Path Orders and Agreements

Countryside (Scotland) Act 1967; Highways Act 1980; Wildlife and Countryside Act 1981. This law applies in England, Wales and Scotland.

A **public path** is created for the benefit to a substantial section of the public or to the convenience of persons living in the area, bearing in mind the effect on the landowner or occupier.

The local planning authority may create a path compulsorily or by agreement with a landowner or tenant. It may be created with or without special conditions. Payment may be involved. There is no set format for the document. Disagreement may be taken to the Secretary of State and compensation may be made.

Other access provisions

- **Public path extinguishment order**
  Paths may be closed without compensation as long as closure does not adversely affect land adjoining the path.

- **Public path diversion order**
  An owner or tenant or occupier can apply for diversion if he or she can demonstrate that there is a more convenient or direct route or prove that such a diversion will result in more efficient use of land.

Long Distance Paths

National Parks and Access to the Countryside Act 1949 and Countryside (Scotland) Act 1981. This law applies in Scotland, England and Wales.

> **Long distance paths** refer to routes recommended by the conservancies along which the public should be allowed to make extensive journeys on foot, pedal cycles or horseback. A route should be for the whole or greater part of its length not along roads used mainly by vehicles.

Detailed proposals are drawn up which have to be approved.

Right to Roam

The Countryside and Rights of Way Act 2000 applies only to England and Wales except in reference to off-the-road use of vehicles and in making clear the relevant legislation for SSSIs in Scotland.

The Act allows any person to enter and remain on any 'access land' for the purposes of open-air recreation, provided that this does not lead to damage to walls, fences, hedges, stiles or gates, or actions deemed to be inappropriate and unlawful, or contravene restrictions. These restrictions are listed in Schedule 2 and some examples are given below.

Under this Act, landowners may not obstruct access, but neither have they been invested with more onerous responsibilities in relation to occupier's liability or risk in general. The Countryside Agency and the Countryside Council for Wales are required to produce maps showing all access land. There is provision for consultation and appeal against designation. Maps must be reviewed within ten years of confirmation. By-laws, wardens and notices indicating boundaries may be established.

> **'Access land'** includes:
> - Open country (mountain, moor, heath or down).
> - Registered common land.
> - Land 600 m above sea level.
> - Especially dedicated land.
> - Coastal land may be included by Order.

> **Excepted land** includes:
> - Land ploughed or drilled in the last 12 months for planting or sowing crops or trees.
> - Land covered by buildings including the curtilage.
> - Land within 20 m of a dwelling.
> - Parks and gardens.
> - Quarries and surface working of minerals.
> - Railways and tramways.
> - Golf course, racecourse or aerodrome.

- Statutory undertakings, telecommunications.
- Land being developed in accordance with the Town and Country Planning Acts.
- Land within 20 m of a permanent building or temporary pens holding livestock.
- Land regularly used for training racehorses.
- Military land.

Restrictions on access include:
- Vehicles other than invalid carriages.
- Bathing or using a vessel or sailboard on non-tidal water.
- Access with animals other than dogs. Dogs must be on a short lead between 1 March and 31 July and at all times when near livestock.
- Criminal acts or intimidation of persons engaged in lawful activity.
- Lighting fires.
- Taking or disturbing flora, fauna or fish, eggs or nests.
- Hunting, shooting or fishing or carrying the apparatus thereof.
- Metal detecting.
- Interference of drains or watercourses.
- Organized games, camping, hang- or paragliding.
- Commercial activity.
- Advertising.

Disability Discrimination Act 1995 (DDA 95)

The **Disability Discrimination Act 1995** makes it unlawful to discriminate against disabled people in normal day-to-day activities. 'Disabled' includes physical and mental disability and facial disfigurement.

Under DDA 95, by the end of 1999 service providers should have amended policies, procedures and practices that prevent service uptake, and also provided additional help (e.g. audiotape for interpretation). By 2000, where reasonable, physical boundaries that prevent access should have been removed or physical access provided in another way.

There are exemptions, including: risk to health and safety; there is only one way to provide services to everyone else; less favourable service permissible only if otherwise impossible to serve disabled people at all; legal duty under other legislation, e.g. listed buildings; national security.

In countryside provision, total *access* to all may be very expensive to provide. The next best option is total *information* so that all may make informed choices about, for example, steepness, steps, route length, transport possibilities, etc. as well as physical provision of route options.

Pollution Control

Public Health (Scotland) Act 1987; Alkali Act 1960; Clean Air Acts 1956–1993; Rivers (Prevention of Pollution) Acts 1951 and 1965; Control of Pollution Act 1974; Water Act 1989; Environmental Protection Act 1990; Environment Act 1995; Noise and Statutory Nuisance Act 1993; Pollution Prevention and Control Act 1999.

Introduction

> Pollution issues may offer employment opportunities for landscape architects through entrust and landfill tax projects or through environmental audit.
>
> Pollution control may impose obligations on clients and affect the management of construction sites. It may also imply a requirement to design surfaces that may be maintained mechanically.

As with planning legislation, statutes about pollution control have arisen from a concern for public health and safety. Early Acts dealt with particular forms of pollution e.g. water, air, litter and ascribed control to separate agencies, but subsequent legislation has consolidated the different statutes and adopted the principle of integrated pollution control (IPC) under fewer but more powerful agencies.

> **Organizations to protect and enhance environmental quality**
>
> Environmental Agency (EA) for England and Wales
> * Created on 1 April 1996 through the Environment Act 1995.
> * Combined the National Rivers Authority, Her Majesty's Inspectorate of Pollution (HMIP) and Waste Regulatory Authorities.
>
> Scottish Environmental Protection Agency (SEPA)
> * Created on 1 April 1996 through the Environment Act 1995.
> * Combined HMIP, the River Purification Boards and the Waste Regulations Authorities and Local Authority Air Pollution Control functions under Part I of the 1990 Environmental Protection Act, although they remain with local authorities in England and Wales.
> * The new independent Water and Sewerage Consumers Council monitors the three water authorities in the north, east and west of Scotland.
> * SEPA, unlike EA, cannot undertake its own legal prosecutions.
>
> Environmental Service in Northern Ireland ES(NI)
> * Responsible for conservation and pollution control.

European Environment Agency
- Established on 30 October 1993.
- Based in Copenhagen.
- Ten tasks concerned with the provision of 'objective, reliable and comparable information at European level' as a basis for environmental protection measures, to assess the results of those measures and to ensure the public is properly informed about the state of the environment.

Integrated Pollution Control

Integrated pollution control is a response to the cross-media movement of pollution and to the case for a unified inspectorate 'to ensure an integrated approach to difficult industrial problems at source, whether these affect air, water or land'. *Air Pollution Control: an integrated approach 1976.*

The principle of IPC was established in statute in the Environmental Protection Act 1990 and fully in force by 1996. (*Refer to website for further details*)

IPC and Planning
Under PPG 23 Planning and Pollution Control, pollution control agencies have the responsibility to advise local planning authorities on pollution aspects of a development. When considering the risk of pollution, planning authorities are to rely on the advice of the pollution control authorities and be aware that 'the perception of risk should not be material to the planning application unless the land use consequences of such perceptions can be clearly demonstrated'.

Pollution Standards

Before IPC was developed, the degree of pollution in the UK was controlled by measurement against various standards. These standards still apply and include specification standards that govern equipment, for instance to arrest grit and dust, emission standards that forbid more than a certain level of emission from a works and receptor standards that restrict activities when these result in a certain level of harm.

Waste

The Environmental Protection Act 1990 created three new agencies: Waste Regulation, Waste Collection and Waste Disposal Authorities.

> **Waste Management Licences** are required from the regulation authority for the disposal, treatment and keeping of waste.
> - Before a licence is granted, consultation is required with the local planning authority (where relevant), the Health and Safety Executive, EA or SEPA, and the relevant nature conservancy if an SSSI is involved.
> - The terms of a licence require control of emission of liquids and gases from landfill sites, both during the filling process and for a number of years following closure.

There is a duty on all those producing, treating or disposing of waste to take all reasonable measures to ensure that there is no unauthorized handling or disposal of their waste.

Waste Regulation Authorities are under a duty to inspect their area for pollution risks caused by past disposal of waste. They should take steps to prevent any pollution or risk to human health, recovering the cost from the occupier of the land unless the authority has accepted the surrender of the relevant licence.

Litter

Environmental Protection Act 1990.

> **The leaving of litter is a criminal offence** and islands and district councils have the power to serve fixed penalty notices on offenders.

Local authorities, educational institutions and statutory undertakers have a duty to ensure that their land is as far as practicable kept clear of litter, and this duty may be enforced by any person aggrieved by the defacement of land by litter seeking an order from the courts.

Landfill Tax

This tax was introduced by the Finance Act 1996 and was further framed by the Landfill Tax Regulations 1996. It applies throughout the United Kingdom.

The tax is levied on material designated as waste deposited on a landfill site on or after 1 October 1996. The tax is paid by the landfill site operator. It is intended to reflect the environmental impact of landfill and to promote more sustainable waste management practices.

What is landfill?

Disposal is considered to be landfill if:

- It is deposited on the surface of the land, on a structure set into the surface or deposited beneath the surface.
- Disposal of material is not taxable if it is obtained by dredging, by dredging for navigational purposes or obtained during the course of sand or gravel extraction from the seabed.
- Deposits are not taxable if they result from commercial mining operations (or are deposits of dead domestic pets!).

Landfill Tax

Currently the tax is levied at £2 a tonne for inert waste, at £11 a tonne for everything else from 1 April 1999, but with planned annual increases of £1 in tax to 2004.

Landfill sites are licensed under the terms of the Environmental Protection Act 1990 and the Pollution Control and Local Government (Northern Ireland) Order 1978.

Environmental Body Tax Credit Scheme and Environmental Trusts

A tax rebate of up to 90 per cent will be deducted from the liability of landfill site operators if they are party to an Environmental Trust for a site. The trusts are to be managed by the local community and registered with the Commissioners for Customs and Excise. Approval and regulation of environmental projects is the responsibility of 'Entrust', an organization established for this purpose.

Environmental Trusts will be formed for purposes that may include:

- Research and development of sustainable waste management practices.
- Collection and dissemination of information about sustainable waste management.
- Remediation and restoration of sites unable to support economic or social activity, harmed previously by waste management or other industrial activities.
- Creation of habitats, wildlife and conservation areas within landfill sites.
- School-based education programmes to raise awareness of waste and its management.

Contaminated Land

Environmental Protection Act 1990 and Part IIA of the Environment Act 1995.

> **Contaminated land** refers to a 'pollution linkage' comprising a source of contamination, a pathway and a receptor. If the pollution linkage is 'significant' the land is classified as statutory contaminated land.

With effect from July 1999, local authorities became required to inspect land within their boundaries for contamination in the form of pollution linkages. The local authority should determine remediation for each pollution linkage. (*Refer to website for further details*)

> **Landscapes, parks and gardens are not considered to be receptors in the definition of pollution linkages.** Therefore damage to vegetation on such sites could not cause land to be classified as contaminated unless humans, animals (livestock, other owned animals, or wild animals subject to shooting or fishing rights) or buildings were also affected.

Abandoned Mines

Following the Environment Act 1995, mine operators now have to give EA or SEPA six months' prior notice of the abandonment of a mine or part of a mine. This should allow EA or SEPA time to plan or advise on anticipated anti-pollution measures, especially pollution of controlled waters by accumulated mine water. This measure is important because mine water may be very toxic and cause serious damage to river life if it escapes.

Statutory Nuisances

The Environmental Protection Act 1990 significantly improved the law of statutory nuisances.

> **Statutory nuisances** (but only when they are prejudicial to health):
> - Smoke.
> - Fumes (including airborne solid matter smaller than dust) or gases.
> - Premises in a state of disrepair.
> - Dust, steam, smell or other effluvia arising on industrial, trade or business premises.
> - Any accumulation or deposit.
> - Noise (which includes vibration) emitted from premises.

Enforcement of the law is the duty of local authorities. They must take action if satisfied that a statutory nuisance exists or is likely to occur or recur. An Abatement Notice will be served on the person responsible, owner or occupier specifying what steps must be taken to deal with the nuisance. This may affect the management of construction sites.

Eco-Management and Audit

Eco-management and audit refers to a voluntary regulation to promote improvements in environmental performance at industrial sites through development of environmental management systems, regular auditing and the provision of information on environmental performance to the public.

This may be a source of work for landscape professionals, because it requires participating companies to identify all significant environmental issues relating to the industrial plant. However, if a landscape/environment practice undertakes an environmental audit their PII must reflect this aspect of work for liability claims.

Key Regulations – Control of Pollution

These are important regulations for landscape architects because it is the landscape architect's responsibility to check that the contractor is complying with all pesticide regulations.

Control of Pesticides Regulations 1986

Control of Pollution Act 1974; Pesticides Act 1998; Biocides Directive.

- Pesticide: a substance for destroying pests, especially insects (includes herbicides, fungicides, wood preservatives, plants and animal repellents and masonry biocides). Also rodenticides and avicides.
- Detailed requirements for aerial application.
- Users to take all reasonable precautions to protect health of human beings, creatures and plants.
- Commercial users must be competent.
- Employers must ensure employees have reached required standard of competence.
- Conditions applied to sale, supply and storage.
- Advertising is controlled.
- Certificate of competence for storing, selling, supplying pesticides required.
- Users to comply with detailed directions for use.
- Listed adjutants (wetting agents) can be used.
- Only certain products can be tank mixed.

Control of Substances Hazardous to Health Regulations 1988 (COSHH)

Control of Pollution Act 1974

The COSHH Regulations require employers, contractors, subcontractors and self-employed people to protect employees who may be exposed to health risks arising from hazardous substances they work with. The Regulations require a written assessment of known risks or hazards and the action required to prevent or to control them.

How COSSH affects landscape architects

- Pesticides (check handling certificate and Certificate of Competence).
- Staining materials.
- Mulch from overseas (check bromide content).

Summary of COSSH requirements

- Assess risks to health from hazardous substances arising in the workplace and determine action needed.
- Implement prevention or control programmes.
- Maintain and monitor those programmes.
- Provide health surveillance where appropriate.
- Inform, instruct and train employees in regard to work with hazardous substances.
- Keep records where required.

COSSH – safety and liability for pesticides

- COSHH assessment is comprehensive – check out all staff fully appraised.
- Check local Water Board.
- Prepare detailed specification and programme.
- Tender documents within requirements of HSE/HSC approved Code of Practice for safe use of pesticides for non-agricultural purposes.

Organization of Countryside and Conservation Authorities

The Environmental Protection Act 1990 split the Nature Conservancy Council (NCC) into three country agencies: English Nature, the Countryside Commission and the Countryside Council for Wales and also established the Joint Nature Conservation Committee. The Countryside Commission and the Rural Development Commission merged in 1999 to become the Countryside Agency. Scottish Natural Heritage was formed in 1991.

Responsibility for the Environment

Organization	Function and responsibility
English Nature	• Nature conservation • Landscape conservation • Countryside recreation • Enhance the countryside • Promote social equity and economic opportunity for countryside occupants • Enjoyment for everyone
Countryside Agency	• Countryside tourism • Biodiversity • Local distinctiveness • Local character in food production • Traffic management • Access • Landscape conservation
Countryside Council for Wales	• Nature conservation • Countryside recreation • Co-ordination between the UK environmental agencies
Joint Nature Conservation Committee	• Provide a national, European and global dimension to nature conservation in the UK.
Scottish Natural Heritage (formerly the Countryside Commission for Scotland and the Nature Conservation Council for Scotland)	• Landscape conservation • Nature conservation • Enjoyment and understanding of the environment • Encourage sustainable use of resources
Farming and Rural Conservation Agency (from April 1997, this agency took over the work formerly carried out by the Agricultural Development and Advisory Service)	• Rural land use planning • Environmental protection • Wildlife management • Conservation • Rural economy
Regional development agencies	• Sustainable development (among other tasks)

Grants

There appear to be many sources of grant for landscape design work. These are summarized in the box and described in more detail on the web.

Grant sources

Grants for landscape conservation including countryside stewardship
- From Scottish Natural Heritage.
- Countryside Agency.
- English Nature.
- Countryside Council for Wales.

Grants for environmental improvements
- Derelict land grants.
- Urban Development grant.
- European Regional Development Funds.
- Sports Council grants.
- Urban Regeneration grant.
- Rural Challenge.
- Millennium Greens.
- Local authority grants.

Grants for habitat creation
- From Countryside Council for Wales.
- English Nature.
- European Union.
- Forestry Authority.
- Forest Company/ Forestry Commission.
- Grant-making trust funds.
- Local authorities.
- DEFRA.
- National Lottery/Millennium Fund.
- Scottish Natural Heritage.
- UK government departments and agencies.
- Corporate grants.

Grants for sustainability
- European Commission LIFE Environment Programme.

5 Tendering

Work Stages

The Landscape Consultant's Appointment describes the preliminary and standard services that a landscape architect will provide from inception to completion for a normal design and implementation project. Work Stages F–H cover Production Information, Bills of Quantities and Tender Action and follows on from the detailed proposals and approvals stage.

Work Stage F: Production Information

Production information can be divided into three aspects describing their function:

> **• Illustrative •**
> Drawings (plans and details)

> **• Qualitative •**
> Specification

> **• Quantitative •**
> Bills of Quantities/Schedules/
> Schedules of Rates

Illustrative: Drawings

Drawings illustrate the layout of the project and the construction of the specified materials. They provide an accurate presentation of the work required in a consistent and clear format to communicate effectively with all members of the design and construction team.

Qualitative: Specification

The specification is a written document that describes the works generally and provides the detailed description of the quality required in terms of construction, workmanship and materials.

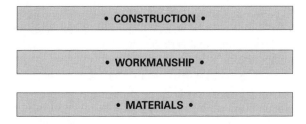

• CONSTRUCTION •

• WORKMANSHIP •

• MATERIALS •

The specification is divided into work sections, which link with the Bills of Quantities (BQ) and drawings. This system is known as the Common Arrangement of Works Section (CAWS), which was set up under the government initiative, Co-ordinated Project Information (CPI), adopted in 1979 for drawings, specification and Bill of Quantities (BQ) aiming to produce a co-ordinated set of documents.

The specification forms part of the contract documents whether individual or contained within the BQ. In the JCLI Form of Agreement it is written into the contract if the specification is a separate contract document or if it forms part of the BQ. Specifications and Bills of Quantities are classified as design under the CDM Regulations.

Methods of specification

Methods of specification are linked to the form of agreement used and there are usually standard systems relating to measurement and specification for each form of agreement

FORM OF AGREEMENT		SPECIFICATION SYSTEM	METHOD OF MEASUREMENT
1	JCT	NBS (National Building Specification)	SMM7

| 2 | ICE | Specification for Road & Bridges Work | CESMM3 |

| 3 | GC WORKS | NBS | SMM7 |

| 4 | JCLI | NBS Landscape | SMM7 |

National standard systems are set up to ensure consistency and accuracy is retained between all elements of the Production Information. Where a non-standard specification system is being used a full descriptive specification can be prepared that is project specific.

EC rules regarding Specifications Directive 89/106/EEC 1988

- All technical specifications shall be defined by reference to national standards implementing European standards (e.g. BSs or ISOs) or by reference to European technical approvals or by reference to common technical specifications.
- Unless justified by the subject of the contract, technical specifications must not mention products of a specific make, source or a particular process. The indication of trade marks, patents, types or of a specific origin or production shall be prohibited unless the phrase 'or equivalent' is used where it is not possible to give a precise enough description of the subject for all parties concerned.

Quantitative: Schedules/Bills of Quantities/Schedules of Rates

Schedules are used to augment the drawings and assist in the preparation of Bills of Quantities. They are used to tabulate information for a range of similar items, such as planting schedules, which list such items as species, type, size, location and unit rate. Bills of Quantities and Schedules of Rates are described more fully below.

Work Stage G: Bills of Quantities

Bills of Quantities act as a link between the design and the implementation of the design. They consist of a list of items describing the works whose total value when priced equals the tender figure. They are prepared according to predetermined rules called Methods of Measurement and can form part of the contract documents.

Purpose
- Enable tenders to be submitted on the same basis.
- Assist the contractor in assessing material, labour and plant requirements.
- Assist in the evaluation of tenders.
- Are a basis for valuing alterations.
- Assist in the preparation of interim valuations.
- Provide information for future estimates.

Layout and contents will vary but generally Bills of Quantities are set out under separate headings.

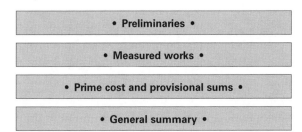

• Preliminaries •

• Measured works •

• Prime cost and provisional sums •

• General summary •

Preliminaries

The preliminaries cover the specific circumstances of the project under which the work will be carried out and which are not covered elsewhere in the tender documents. They comprise a list of items affecting the works as a whole, which are priced by the contractor, and these costs are carried forward to the general summary. The preliminaries form the backbone of the contractor's understanding of the working arrangements of the project and may influence their tender price.

Preliminaries
- Site description.
- Access and egress.
- Site security.
- Statutory approvals.
- Team accommodation/equipment requirements.
- Site meetings.
- Disturbance to third parties (noise, dust, cleaning of roads, access over land, temporary road closures).
- Warranties and bonds.
- Quality checks and samples.

- Health and safety.
- Programme.
- Valuation and payment dates.
- Record drawings.
- Guarantees.
- Dayworks.

Payments for these items are due in the month/valuation period that they are expended. Normally they are paid as a proportion of the contract duration as it is unusual for the contractor to provide a breakdown of each item in his tender price.

Dayworks

These are works that cannot properly be measured and priced in accordance with the Bill of Quantities and therefore have to be dealt with on a labour, materials and plant basis, plus percentage for profit and overheads.
- Current agreed national rates for construction workers are used to value labour costs.
- Materials are valued as actual cost.
- There are set rates for plant costs published by the RICS and ICE. The method used should be stated in the dayworks section of the BQ.
- The tenderer states his percentage profit in the dayworks section of the BQ.

Measured Works

This is the 'quantities' section of the Bill of Quantities and summarizes information from the drawings and specification. It is prepared in accordance with predetermined Methods of Measurement (Methods of Measurement relate to how items are quantified and how the Bill of Quantities is laid out) to produce a national general standard.

Four Rules of Measurement

- Civil engineers' standard method of measurement (CESMM).
- Standard method of measurement of building works (SMM7).
- Code for the measurement of building works in small dwellings.
- Method of measurement for road and bridge works.

SMM is based on the Co-ordinating Committee for Project Information (CCPI) Common Arrangement, adopted also for drawings and specifications, (e.g. NBS) to produce a co-ordinated set of documents.

Measurement is approached systematically through each work section (earthworks, topsoiling, cultivations, seeding, planting). Any departures from the standard measurement conventions must be specifically drawn to the attention of the tenderer.

Prime Cost, Provisional and Contingency Sums

Prime Cost Sum

A sum of money allowed in the Bill of Quantities for works, goods or services to be carried out or supplied by either the contractor, nominated subcontractor or nominated supplier for which the details are known at the time of tender.

Prime cost sum

- An exact sum of money specified for an exact piece of work.
- When the contractor tenders he will allow in his rates the sum given in the Bill of Quantities plus his detailed profit and special attendance costs.

Provisional Sum

A sum allowed in the Bill of Quantities for works or goods that cannot be accurately quantified or detailed entirely at the time the tender documents are issued. The contractor allows the sum plus percentage profit, except with JCLI form of agreement where no percentage is allowed for profit. Provisional sums are identified under SMM7 as either defined work or undefined work.

Provisional sum

Defined Work

Work not completely designed but includes information on:
- The nature and construction of the work.
- Approximate quantities that indicate the scope and extent of the work.

In this instance the contractor will be deemed to have made due allowance in his programming, planning and pricing of the preliminaries.

Undefined Work

Work where no information is available. The contractor will not be deemed to have made any allowance in his programming, planning and pricing of preliminaries.

Contingency Sum

A sum allowed in the Bill of Quantities for works or costs required as a result of that which could not have been foreseen or accounted for. A contingency sum can only be expended in part or whole on the written authority of the landscape architect e.g. soft spots at formation, reclamation, drainage. The sum can be expressed in two ways:

Contingency Sum

• A specific sum entered in the Bill of Quantities.
• A sum calculated on a specific percentage of the contractor's tender (2.5–5 per cent).

General Summary

This is the summary of costs from each section of the Bill of Quantities. The total of the general summary is the tender figure, which is carried to the 'form of tender'.

Schedules of Rates

Schedules of Rates are used where the actual quantities of work required are not known at the outset and are remeasured and valued only when it has been completed.

A comprehensive Schedule of Rates including all that is likely to be required may often be little less than a Bill of Quantities without the quantities. In this situation approximate quantities can be included that are based on approximation of the area or volume envisaged. Although the work must be remeasured on completion the tender rates quoted are more likely to be accurate.

A Schedule of Rates can be used alongside a fixed quoted lump sum for the works (usually with very small projects using JCT Minor Works Contract). The schedule will be used to value any additional works over that for which the lump sum has been quoted.

A Schedule of Rates can be used for serial tendering/measured-term contracts.

The Quantity Surveyor

The quantity surveyor is employed when the service he renders will be of value and economic with respect to the project. This should be for large contracts where proper cost control is essential. The quantity surveyor is employed either by the client or by the landscape architect and is paid directly by the client or has their cost included in the landscape architect's fee.

> **Role of quantity surveyor (pre-contract)**
> - Prices landscape architect's proposed scheme to enable the employer to compare all the aspects of the designs.
> - Prepares the Bill of Quantities by extracting the amounts of work from the landscape architect's drawings and specifications.
> - Prepares pre-tender probable costs.
> - Checks the priced Bills of Quantities submitted by the lowest tenderer.
> - Reports to client via landscape architect on the tenders recommended for acceptance or not.
> - Amends or negotiates with the lowest tenderer.

Work Stage H: Tender Action

Types of Tender

A tender is the price for which the tenderer (contractor) offers to carry out and complete, in accordance with the conditions of the contract and statutory requirements, the works shown on the drawings and described in the Bills of Quantities and/or specification.

There are two main types of tendering, non-competitive and competitive, although some types of tendering combine aspects of both. Within each of these types there are different methods of obtaining tenders.

> **• COMPETITIVE •**
> Open
> Selective (single or two stage)
> Serial

> **• NON-COMPETITIVE •**
> Nominated
> Negotiated (single or two stage)

Competitive Tendering

Open Tendering

Anyone is invited to apply to tender for the contract. Advertisements can be put in the press and tender documents are issued to those applying, normally on receipt of a deposit, which is refunded when a tender is returned.

A European Directive covers requirements of tendering public works or supply contracts Europe-wide to achieve competition. It requires tenders expected to be over a certain value to be advertised in a Europe-wide tender journal inviting offers. The threshold value is stated in

ECUs excluding VAT and is subject to regular amendment. The final selection of tenderers can, however, be by selection, negotiation or open tendering depending on the individual client and their own governing regulations.

Single Stage Selective Tendering

The Code of Procedure for Single Stage or Two Stage Selective Tendering published by the National Joint Consultative Committee for Building (NJCC) set out the rules that govern selective tendering, which should be adhered to in order to obtain fair and competitive tenders. They do not, however, have to be followed unless it is stated in the tender documents that they are to be used. (*See 'Procedure for single stage selective tendering' below*)

A shortlist of tenderers is drawn up and they are issued with a set of tender documents for pricing. The object of selection is to make a list of firms, any one of which could be entrusted with the job. If this is achieved, then the final choice of contractor will be simple – the firm offering the lowest tender. Only the most exceptional cases justify departure from this general recommendation.

Two Stage Selective Tendering

This form of tendering is normally used where it is thought that there will be a benefit in having the contractor appointed early in the design process. This could be to take advantage of particular skills the contractor possesses to develop the design, or because the design and construction phase are to overlap. It also allows the selected contractor to become involved in the planning and development of the project.

First stage

- Bills of Approximate Quantities and outline design information are provided to a number of tenderers for pricing in accordance with the NJCC Code.

Second stage

- Negotiation based on the information provided at tender stage. The design team and the selected contractor collaborate in finalizing the design and development of production drawings, the health and safety plan and the Bills of Quantities for the works, which will result in a final agreed sum for the works.
- Once agreement on the contract sum has been agreed a contract can be completed between the contractor and client.

Serial Tendering

Serial tendering is a combination of competitive and non-competitive tendering often used where there will be a number of similar repeat contracts. The contractor tenders for a project knowing that, if their performance is satisfactory, they will be awarded subsequent contracts.

The contract sum for the subsequent contracts will be negotiated from the original tender, updated for any fluctuations in labour rates, materials, fuel, tax etc. since the date of the tender. It is suitable where a number of similar projects will follow on from each other such as streetscape enhancement within a town centre where similar materials and details are used. The similarity of the works produces a learning curve for the contractor providing the client with time and cost savings.

Non-competitive Tendering

Nominated Tendering

One contractor is nominated for the job. This typically occurs where the client has a preference for a particular contractor due to work previously carried out or if the project requires a particular specialism that the contractor can offer. As competition is eliminated the price will normally be higher than that obtained through competition.

If recommending this form of tendering the landscape architect must be sure the benefits outweigh the potential additional cost to the client as it is very rare to have a totally nominated tender, most will be by negotiation.

Negotiated Tendering (single stage and two stage)

The contract price is negotiated between the client (or quantity surveyor if appointed) and the contractor.

> **Use of negotiated tendering**
>
> - The contractor has an established working relationship with a client.
> - Time for construction is limited.
> - There are specialized building techniques involved and the contractor's expertise could be valuable.
> - A project involves additional work.

Single Stage Negotiation

To speed up the procedure of negotiation the contractor will normally price the tender documents and forward them to the QS (quantity surveyor) for checking. The QS will check the rates and prices within the tender documents noting any contentious items. These will be the items discussed during the negotiation stage, all other items being accepted as priced. When agreement on all the items is reached a contract will be entered into based on the revised, negotiated tender sum.

Two Stage Negotiation

Two stage negotiation attempts to introduce some of the advantages of competitive tendering by obtaining tenders from a number of selected contractors. The tenders will consist of an ad hoc selection of rates for the major items of work e.g. bulk excavations, topsoil, together with a priced preliminaries section, an outline programme and samples of all in labour rates, plant rates and materials prices expected to be used on the contract. On the basis of these rates and, in most cases, an interview, a preferred bidder will be selected and negotiation similar to single stage will take place based on the rates already provided.

Two stage negotiation is often used to select a management contractor or where it is important to have a contractor on board before all the design work is completed.

Advantages and Disadvantages of Alternative Types of Tendering

Selective Tendering

Advantages
- This process reduces abortive aggregated costs of estimating.
- Tenderers should be capable of the works and in a favourable financial situation.
- Tenderers have confidence that they are in a group facing similar conditions.

Disadvantages
- Cost level of tenders tends to be slightly higher due to better quality of tenderers and reduced competition.
- Possibility of malpractice due to price fixing (there are still a few sectors of the industry and geographical locations where 'cartels' exist).

Open Tendering

Advantages
- Competitive prices are usually obtained.
- Provides opportunities for firms wishing to diversify.
- Eliminates potential malpractice and price-fixing rings.
- Eliminates the potential charge of favouritism on a client.

Disadvantages

- Lowest tender may be submitted by a contractor inexperienced in tendering who therefore made a number of errors.
- Lowest tenderer may be unsuitable for the type of project or be financially unsound. Obtaining references may offset this slightly.
- Total cost of tendering is increased as all tenderers have to recoup costs eventually in successful tenders.

Negotiated Tendering

Advantages

- Useful when time is limited and an early appointment of contractor is desired.
- Allows potential cost or time savings by using the contractor's expertise and skills during the design development and planning stage.
- Useful when client/design team and contractor have an established relationship.

Disadvantages

- Leads to higher pricing.

Procedure for Single Stage Selective Tendering

(Refer to Code of Procedure for Single Stage Selective Tendering published by the National Joint Consultative Committee for Building (NJCC) January 1996.)
   This process is orientated towards JCT-type contracts. The Institute of Civil Engineers do have separate tendering procedure for use with ICE-type contracts.

Shortlist

A shortlist of tenderers is drawn up and a maximum of six tenderers for each project chosen. If there is likely to be extensive quantification, specification, specialization and calculation then it should be a maximum of four. (The Code of Procedure for Single Stage Selective Tendering, the National Joint Consultative Committee for Building, January 1996.)

Shortlist

- Location of the firm.
- Financial standing and record.
- The firm's general experience, skill and reputation in the area in question.

- Adequacy of the firm's technical and management structure for the type of contract envisaged.
- The firm's competence and resources in respect of statutory health and safety requirements.
- The firm's approach to quality assurance systems.
- Whether the firm will have adequate capacity at time of tender.

Preliminary Inquiry

Either the standard letter contained within Appendix A of the Code can be used (different for each type of contract) or telephone. Four to six preliminary inquiries should be made before the formal invitation to tender to allow contractors to decide if they are in a position to tender or not.

Formal Invitation to Tender

All tenderers are issued with the same information for tender purposes.

Information issued to tenderers
- A formal invitation to tender by letter (see Appendix B of Code).
- Two copies of the form of tender (Appendix C of the Code).
- Two copies of the drawings.
- Two copies of the Bill of Quantities/specification/schedules.
- Addressed tender return envelope.
- Instructions to tenderer – regarding inspection of sites, tendering procedure, conditions of contract, adjustment of priced bills, date and time for return of tender etc.
- CDM questionnaire (covering contractor's understanding of his duties with respect to health and safety, in-house procedures and arrangements should there be an accident etc.).
- Two copies of the pre-tender stage health and safety plan produced by the planning supervisor including risk assessments from all designers.
- Anything else particular to that contract.

Tender Return

A minimum of four working weeks should be allowed for the return of tenders (depending on size and complexity of job). ICE-type contracts allow for a pre-tender meeting and site inspection to discuss the site and the works with all the tenderers.

Tender return procedure
- Tenders are opened at a specific time stated in the invitation to tender (usually 12 noon).

- In Scotland Bills of Quantities are submitted as a whole within the tender return. In England just the price of the tender is submitted but following this the lowest tenderer is given four days to submit the Bill for checking.
- A list of openings is prepared and witnessed (one in England and two in Scotland).
- In local authorities, tenders go to the Chief Executive. The chairman of the committee that authorizes funding of the project signs the tenders and accepts them subject to checking. The professional then does all the checking of tenders.
- Tenders received after time should not be admitted to the competition.

Checking of Tenders

In England the lowest tender is submitted and checked only. (Only if there are arithmetical errors are the second and third lowest bills requested).

In Scotland the three lowest tenders are arithmetically checked before rates are checked for any anomalies. Any obvious errors are recorded.

Qualification of Tender

Tenderers should not attempt to vary the identical basis of the tender by qualifying their tender. A tenderer who submits a qualified tender should be given the opportunity to withdraw the qualification without amendment to his tender; if he fails to do so his tender is rejected.

Errors in Tender Prices

Tenderers sometimes make mistakes in their tender prices. The quantity surveyor or landscape architect will check each item (rate and price) of the tenders. If the NJCC Code of Procedure is used then errors will be dealt with using one of the two alternatives specified in the formal Invitation to Tender and the Form of Tender.

Alternative 1: confirm or withdraw

The tenderer is informed of the errors and given the opportunity to confirm or withdraw his offer. This does not allow for the tender figure reported to the client to be amended and the figure remains the same.
- If the tenderer withdraws, then the second lowest tender is checked.
- If the tenderer confirms the tender as it stands, then an endorsement is added to the priced Bill of Quantities. This indicates that all rates or prices (excluding preliminary items, contingencies, prime cost and

provisional sums) are considered reduced or increased in the same proportion as the corrected total of priced items exceeds or falls short of such items. Both the client and tenderer sign the endorsement.

Alternative 2: confirm, amend or withdraw

The tenderer is given the opportunity to confirm his offer or amend it to correct genuine errors. This allows for the tender figure to be amended.
- If the tenderer confirms, Alternative 1 procedure is followed.
- If the tenderer chooses to amend his offer, the new price is checked to ensure that it does not exceed the next lowest tender. If it does the new lowest tender is checked.
- If the amended price is still the lowest tender, the tenderer has to be allowed access to his original Bill of Quantities to correct the details and initial them. Or he will be required to confirm all the alterations in a letter. If he is subsequently successful in his tender this letter should be joined with the acceptance and the amended tender figure and the rates in it substituted for those in the original tender.

Tender Report and Recommendation

Tender report contents
- A statement of what the project comprises and the form of tendering used.
- The list of the tenderers and an explanation of any tenders not made or withdrawn.
- The range of tender prices.
- A note of obvious errors and the modifications made as a result.
- Amendments made to the tender documents during the tender period.
- In Scotland a detailed comparison of prices for the three lowest tenders (comparison of day work rates, preambles, preliminaries and prime cost sums).
- A comment on rates in the context of the present state of the market.
- Confirmation that tenders were fairly, accurately and consistently priced.
- Recommendation.

Usually the lowest tender is recommended for acceptance. Only in exceptional circumstances should the landscape architect recommend other than the lowest tender because all are supposed to be suitable.

If tenders are over budget the tender report can incorporate a statement of any savings that could be made to bring the lowest tender within budget. A bill of reductions can be produced after negotiation with the lowest tenderer.

Acceptance of Tender

The tender report is sent to the client with a request for approval of the recommendation. If the client accepts, then either the client or the landscape architect on his behalf writes to the tenderer accepting his offer. This acceptance of an offer initiates a contract.

Post-Tender Period

Notification of Tenders

Once the contract has been let every tenderer should be supplied with a list of the firms who tendered (in alphabetical order) and a list of the tender prices (in ascending order of value).

Contract Preparation

Upon receipt of the letter of acceptance from the client or landscape architect, all documents become contract documents and the tenderer becomes the contractor. All the contract documents are signed and witnessed (two witnesses in Scotland).

NJCC recommend that the lowest tenderer only should be required to submit a response to the health and safety plan and this should be done as soon as possible. The CDM Regulations state that the contractor cannot commence work until the Health and Safety Executive has been notified (Form F10) and the contractor's construction stage health and safety plan approved by the planning supervisor.

6 Contract and Contract Administration

Standard Forms of Agreement

Standard forms of contract exist for the following reasons:

> **CERTAINTY**
>
> The required performance of each party involved in the contract is known and clearly stated.
>
> **STANDARDIZATION**
>
> Wide use of standard forms enables contractors and professionals to be familiar with the rules laid down. This saves time, helps avoid confusion and provides a tried and tested framework for the successful completion of a contract.
>
> **SUITED FOR PURPOSE**
>
> There are several standard forms of agreement. Each has been designed for particular kinds of project. Part of the professional's job is to choose the appropriate form of agreement for the job in hand.

All standard contracts comprise the following:

> • **THE AGREEMENT** •
> +
> • **SPECIFICATION** •
> +
> • **SCHEDULE OR BILL OF QUANTITIES** •
> +
> • **DRAWINGS** •
> +
> • **CONTRACT FORM** •

The Agreement includes the Parties (parties to the contract are named), Recitals (identifying the project; the items that form the contract documents, including the conditions of contract, name of the quantity surveyor if used and reference to the warranty, Articles (stating in principle what each of the parties to the contract will do), and Witnesses to the agreement.

The specification is information about the quality of materials and standard of workmanship; the schedule or Bill of Quantities is the quantitative information required; and the drawings are the illustrative information. The form of agreement or contract form is chosen to suit the type of work being carried out.

Types of Contract

There are a number of different types of contract. Some of these are described below:

> **'FIXED PRICE/LUMP SUM'**
> **'COST REIMBURSEMENT'**
> **'ALL IN'**
> **'MANAGEMENT'**

The landscape architect, whilst required to be aware of the different types of contract, will in most cases only use fixed price contracts.

Fixed Price/Lump Sum Contract

With Bills of Quantities

This is the method usually used for landscape works. Advantages of this method are:

- Tenderers are able to state the total costs involved.
- All tenderers are pricing using the same quantities.
- All tenders should be exactly comparable.

With Schedule of Rates

This is a pre-priced schedule of items with no quantities where all the expected work is covered and the tenderer inserts his plussage or percentage against it. The schedule is often broken down into sections. Used where speed is important and where it is not possible to quantify what is involved, or a purpose prepared schedule where work for a defined area or aspect is given in the form of a list of items and approximate quantities. The tenderer prices it in full. The approximate or notional quantities are replaced by Bills of Firm Quantities later. Used when haste is required or for a series of broadly similar jobs i.e. serial tendering.

Lump sum

A price based on drawings and specification, usually used for minor projects.

The Cost Reimbursement Contract

(Also known as Cost Plus or Measurement Contracts.)

This type of contract is used in extreme urgency. The selection of a good contractor is important, usually chosen by negotiated tender. These contracts carry a heavy penalty for the client as the administrative costs are usually high.

'Prime cost' here means the direct cost of labour, equipment (plant) fuel and materials required for the job.

The contractor undertakes to do an indeterminate amount of work for a sum of money to be ascertained on the basis of actual costs incurred. The fee includes overheads and profit.

Prime cost plus percentage fee

The percentage fee covers any indirect charges that the contractor wishes to make. There is no real incentive for the contractor to work efficiently. Usually used where requirements are difficult to ascertain pre-contract.

Prime cost plus fixed fee

Fixed fee is based on an estimated cost of the project. The fee is fixed by the contractor at tender stage. Used where the amount of work can be estimated reasonably well. The contractor has an incentive to work in order to remain within his fee. Requires very careful cost estimating.

Prime cost plus fluctuating fee

The size of the fee relates to the prime cost. If the contractor's prime costs are high, he receives a low fee and vice versa. The contractor has an incentive to work efficiently.

The Target Cost Contract

A combination of prime costs and percentage fee and a scheduled contract. Any difference between the target cost and the actual prime cost is split between the employer and the contractor.

The All In Contract

A contract where the contractor takes on the whole design and construct elements of the contract, used to eliminate conflicts of interest in the team. The contractor provides the full service including design and construction.

> **ALL IN CONTRACTS**
>
> **ADVANTAGES**
> * Building contractor responsible for whole contract.
> * Costs (including securing planning consents) and building regulations taken on by contractor.
> * Single point of contract for client.
> * Effective completion on time and costs.
>
> **DISADVANTAGES**
> * Costs are utmost.
> * Quality of design is hard to safeguard.

The Management Contract

The contractor is appointed to manage the construction of a contract. This is used when the completion date is so important that the work on site must start before the client's requirements and design is finalized and costs ascertained.

Forms of Agreement/Contract

Listed below are some of the main forms of agreement used by landscape architects.

> * ICE *
>
> * NEC *
>
> * GC WORKS *
>
> * JCT *
>
> * JCT MINOR *
>
> * JCT INTERMEDIATE *
>
> * JCLI *

(Refer to the website for recent changes to legislation, which have affected all contracts)

ICE Form (Institute of Civil Engineers)

Designed for large civil engineering contracts (i.e. bridges, motorways, slag heaps, sewage works etc.). A very simple form for a few trades with wide powers i.e. engineer can dictate sequence of execution, simple quantities. All work is remeasured as it proceeds and therefore the final price is uncertain. The contractor is entitled to extensions of time and extra payment if he encounters physical conditions or artificial obstructions not reasonably foreseen by an experienced contractor.

New Engineering and Construction Contract

The Institute of Civil Engineers also produced the NEC (New Engineering Contract). NEC represents a very different approach to contracts and to working within a contract.

GC Works – Government Contracts

GC Works/1, for major building and civil engineering work, is in three versions: with quantities; without quantities; single stage design and build.

- GC/Works/2 for minor building and civil engineering work.
- GC/Works/3 for mechanical and electrical engineering.
- GC/Works/4 for small building, civil, mechanical and electrical work.
- GC/Works/5 procurement of professional services.

JCT Standard Form of Building Contract (Joint Contracts Tribunal)

Incorrectly also known as the RIBA form. Now a very complex document in a variety of forms: i.e. with/without quantities, private/local authority; approximate quantities; phased completion variants. Used for building contracts of approximately £500 000 and over. Various forms for nominated subcontractors (NSC) are used with JCT and are discussed later in this chapter.

JCT Intermediate

This also known as IFC (Intermediate Form of Contract). Slightly simpler than JCT. There is no nomination of subcontractors, just 'naming'. Suitable for contracts of less than 12 months.

JCT Minor Building Works

Designed for use on relatively low value private or local authority, new and amended fixed price contracts. Very useful for a wide variety of projects including landscape, except it lacks the clauses for variations, objections to a nomination, penultimate certificate, fluctuations, and malicious damage or theft that are included in the JCLI form.

This form is much simpler and easier to understand than JCT. Involving less administration, it is also cheaper to use than JCT. However, some clauses are omitted and therefore certain matters are undefined e.g. there are no provisions for extensions of time and the valuation of variations is uncertain. There is no provision for nominated subcontractors and therefore it is not appropriate where specialist subcontractors are required.

JCT Intermediate Landscape Supplement

A supplement to the JCT Intermediate Form with provision for increased costs, vandalism, dead plants and partial possession by the employer.

JCLI (Joint Council for Landscape Industries)

In 1998 the JCLI (Joint Council of Landscape Industries) form of agreement was updated and split into the two following contracts.

JCLI Landscape Works '98

There are several fundamental differences to the previous version of the contract:

- There is no provision for maintenance after completion and a separate JCLI agreement for landscape maintenance works is available for this purpose.
- Provision has been included in the document to allow the release of retentions as various defects periods expire.

The JCLI form of contract is a very simple contract originally based mainly on the JCT minor works contract. It does allow for nominated subcontractors, the Penultimate Certificate, malicious damage or theft and fluctuations, but more importantly it allows for options regarding plant defects liability and post–practical completion by the employer or contractor. (*Refer to the website for details of the landscape architect's duties*)

JCLI Landscape Maintenance Agreement '98

The JCLI agreement for Maintenance Works '98 is appropriate for use in two different circumstances:

- With a construction contract to cover maintenance during the planting defects period.
- For the landscape maintenance works not associated with a construction contract.

The contract allows for periodic payments and annual accounts. A bonus scheme can be applied for completion of work as programmed. Liquidated damages can be applied to items not carried out by the contractor on time or in accordance with specification.

If a landscape architect wishes to provide a contract for both landscape and maintenance works the two documents must be used and should be tendered together and signed at the same time.

Subcontracts

There are usually two types of subcontract:

> **• NOMINATED SUBCONTRACTS •**
> OR
> **• DOMESTIC SUBCONTRACTS •**

Nominated subcontracts

The landscape architect nominates the subcontractor when specialist techniques are required, early ordering is necessary and work of a particular quality is essential.

With nominated subcontracts either a single firm is nominated within the document or a list of subcontractors is given.

In both cases, either before letting the main contract or during its early stages, the landscape architect invites tenders from a number of firms he thinks capable of performing the nominated subcontractor works. Then he instructs the main contractor to accept a firm as a nominated subcontractor.

The conditions of contract for the subcontractor must be no more or less onerous than those binding the main contractor and the client. This applies to insurances too.

Several forms known by the letters NSC (nominated subcontractor) are used in association with JCT:

- **NSC/T**   Standard form of nominated subcontractor tender.
  Three parts: Invitation.
  Tender.
  Conditions.

- **NSC/A** Agreement between nominated subcontractor and contractor.
- **NSC/N** A nomination instruction.
- **NSC/C** Standard conditions of nominated subcontract.
- **NSC/W** Employer and nominated subcontractor agreement.

If a nominated subcontractor delays completion of the works, the main contractor is entitled to an extension of time. Equally the client suffers a loss of right to apply liquidated and ascertained damaged if a delay is due to a nominated subcontractor.

Payment of Nominated Subcontractors
It is usually stipulated that subcontractors must be paid within 14 days of certified completion of their works.

If the nominated subcontractor is not paid, the landscape architect is entitled to raise this issue with the main contractor . If there is no action by the main contractor then the landscape architect advises the client to pay the subcontractor directly and issue certificates directly to the subcontractor.

Domestic Subcontracts

With domestic subcontracts the contractor chooses the subcontractor and is responsible in all ways. He lists the subcontractor in the tender and the landscape architect may have the right to disapprove him.

The landscape architect will have nothing to do with a domestic subcontractor and is not responsible for payments to the subcontractor. The contractor and subcontractor usually have a good working relationship.

Named Subcontractors

Specific to IFC. The firm you require to do the work is named in the specification. The contractor enters a subcontract with the named firm. The contractor has the right to object to the named firm. The subcontractor becomes a domestic subcontractor.

Roles of People Engaged in landscape contracts

The parties to a landscape contract will be the client and the contractor. In normal procurement situations there are the following teams (these are different for Design and Build Contracts):

> **THE DESIGN TEAM**
>
> Client
> Landscape architect or contract administrator
> The project manager
> Quantity surveyor
> Other consultants
> The clerk of works
> The planning supervisor
>
> **THE CONTRACTOR**
>
> The contracts manager
> Site agent/foreman
> H&S representative
> Subcontractors

Of its members the client, the landscape architect, the quantity surveyor, the contractor, the nominated subcontractor and the clerk of works are all mentioned in most standard contracts. Other consultants are not and their position will depend largely on what form of agreement they have with the client or the landscape architect.

The Client

A private client may be unaware of the sequence of the design and construction process or of the functions and responsibilities of those engaged in a landscape contract. He also has additional responsibilities under CDM Regulations. The landscape architect, as the client's agent, should advise him of his role.

The client as the employer will be responsible for the following:

- Either decide the functions that the scheme is to fulfil or instruct the landscape architect to investigate these functions and thereafter agree them with him.
- Decide the approximate outlay that can be expended.
- Appoint a landscape architect; also a quantity surveyor and a clerk of works or other professionals if required.
- Sign the legal agreement or contract, which contains the clauses governing the conduct of the parties to the contract, namely the employer and the contractor.
- It is the client's duty to appoint a competent planning supervisor and principal contractor under the CDM Regulations and ensure that sufficient resources will be allocated to enable the work to be carried out safely.
- During the course of and at the end of the contract the employer will pay any money due for services directly to the contractor, the amount

being shown on certificates issued by the landscape architect, and in the time specified in the contract.

WHAT SHOULD THE CLIENT BE AWARE OF?

* His responsibilities and obligations, including adherence to these in a timely manner.
* Terms of engaging a professional person and the methods of working.
* Delegation of responsibility to the professional person as his agent.

The Landscape Architect/Contract Administrator

The landscape architect is the agent of the employer and is either appointed by the employer directly or as a consultant to an architect or engineer who is an appointee of the employer. The landscape architect is required, in accordance with *The Landscape Consultant's Appointment* or his agreement with the client, to:

* Advise the client on the appointment of the contractor and the responsibilities of the client, the contractor and the landscape consultant under the terms of the contract documents.
* Prepare the contract documents and arrange for them to be signed by the client and the contractor and provide production information as required by the contract.
* Administer the contract during operations on site including control of the clerk of works where appointed.
* Visit the site at intervals appropriate to the contractor's programmed activities to inspect the progress and quality of the works.
* Check and certify the authenticity of accounts.
* Make periodic financial reports to the client, identify any variation in the cost of the works or in the expected duration of the contract.
* Ensure the client understands his responsibility regarding CDM Regulations including notifiable work and the appointment of a planning supervisor.
* Carry out all design and specification work in accordance with CDM Regulations and prepare a Risk Assessment. Provide information to the planning supervisor.

The Project Manager

For larger, more complex projects, a project manager is employed by the client. Project management is defined as the overall planning, co-ordination and control of the project from inception to completion. The key role is to motivate, manage, co-ordinate and maintain the morale of the whole project team. The project manager is responsible for:

- Acting on behalf of and representing the client.
- Providing a cost effective and independent service.
- Managing different disciplines and expertise.
- Satisfying the objectives and provisions of the project brief from inception to completion.

The Quantity Surveyor – Contract Period

(The responsibilities of a QS in the pre-contract period are covered in Chapter 5.)

The quantity surveyor will be responsible for:

- Measuring work carried out on site and valuing any materials held on site, at intervals.
- Agreeing, with the contractor's representative, the value of the interim measurement.
- Preparing and submitting these valuations to the landscape architect, who will use the figures to prepare interim certificates.
- Giving estimates of the cost of additional work involved and also of any consequential savings of work omitted because of variation orders.
- Agreeing the value of such work with the contractor.
- If requested, preparing variation Bill of Quantities to cover such work.
- Measuring and calculating the value of work carried out, and agreeing this value with the contractor on completion of the work.
- Submitting the valuation to the landscape architect.
- Generally advising the landscape architect of financial aspects and implications of the labour and material costs, insurance charges etc. involved in any design or change of design in construction.

The Clerk of Works

The clerk of works is engaged by either the client or the landscape architect. He will work under the supervision of the landscape architect and his duties will include the following:

- Maintain a register of drawings and all contract documentation.
- Notify the landscape architect of any errors or discrepancies in the contract documents.
- Notify the landscape architect immediately of any significant problems on site, or if any decisions or variations are required.
- Inspect materials and goods for compliance with the stated standards and see that they are properly stored and protected. Inspect delivery notes and obtain necessary certificates.

- Inspect work for execution in accordance with the contract documents and with instruction or variation orders; witness and record any tests.
- Issue verbal instructions. They must be confirmed in writing by the landscape architect within two days.
- Maintain a daily diary recording such things as weather, instructions issued, details of attendance at dayworks, labour on site, delays, records of any tests.
- Submit weekly reports on the state and progress of the works completed with the master programme.
- Attend site progress meetings and confirm accuracy of the contractor's progress report.
- Observe health and safety requirements with particular reference to CDM Regulations.
- Measure/inspect work that may be buried if required.

A BUILDING CLERK OF WORKS

If you are working with a clerk of works who knows about building but not about landscape work:

- Go through the drawings, bills and specification with him to make sure he understands what is involved and what is important.
- Show him what a sample of good quality topsoil looks like.
- Have all plants delivered to the site labelled by species or at least have a labelled sample of each species to hand for comparison or ensure that you have checked them or tagged them at the nursery.

The Planning Supervisor

The planning supervisor has overall responsibility for:

- Co-ordinating the health and safety aspects of the design and planning phase and for the early stages of the health and safety plan and the health and safety file.
- Ensuring the principal contractor registers with the HSE for construction work that is notifiable.

Other Consultants

Consultants act purely as advisers to the landscape architect on specialist aspects of design or construction. They act under the landscape architect and cannot issue instructions directly. Evidence of consultants PII should be sent to the landscape architect's insurers for verification.

The Main Contractor

The contractor enters into a legal agreement with the client and signs the contract document. He will be responsible for:

- Carrying out and completing the work in accordance with the contract documents and to the satisfaction of the landscape architect.
- Providing materials, goods and workmanship in accordance with the contract documents.
- Complying with statutory requirements and local by-laws.
- Ensuring that all the requirements of necessary legislation and regulations such as HASAW, CDM and Building Regulations are complied with – such as registering with HSE for notifiable work, training for employees in health and safety and ensuring that adequate funds are made available for health and safety.
- Appointing an H&S officer and preparing the health and safety plan in accordance with CDM Regulations. Ensuring that other subcontractors carry out a risk assessment of operations on site. Providing information for the health and safety file.
- Complying with the landscape architect's instructions or variations.
- Providing appropriate insurances and certificates.
- Organizing the sequence of the works and preparing the detailed programme.
- Co-ordinating the works of all subcontractors and suppliers.
- Keeping a competent person in charge of the works.
- Giving notice of expected delays and the reasons for them.
- Making good any defects.
- Payment of wages/deduction of income tax for all employees.

Site Agent/Foreman/Manager

The site agent is the contractor's representative and will be responsible for all items listed under the main contractor applied to the working of the site and also for the following:

- Taking charge of the drawings, specification, Bill of Quantities etc.
- Layout of site including any plant and huts.
- Organizing the labour teams, and day-to-day running of the site.
- Supervision of the work.
- Phasing the delivery of materials.
- Receiving instruction from the landscape architect.
- Presentation of the firm's policy to the workers.
- Feeding back information to the firm.
- Feeding back any complaints he cannot deal with.
- Probably the most important – showing a profit on each site.

HOW TO OBTAIN GOOD QUALITY IN A LANDSCAPE JOB

Contract running is an important part of design work.
Be meticulous, careful and accurate in running a job.
Keep a diary, correspondence, minutes.
You must provide time for contract administration.
You must create the right atmosphere to get the best possible job.
Remember quality starts on the drawing board.
Relations with the contractor are important.
Use a clerk of works.
Use samples of workmanship or materials to guard against you and the contractor having different understandings about the specification.

The Pre-Start/Pre-Contract Meeting

When the contractor has been appointed by the client and the contract placed, an initial project meeting with the contractor and all others concerned should be arranged prior to works commencing on site. The meeting is held to establish contract procedure and administration and is usually chaired by the landscape architect (contract administrator). An agenda should be issued prior to the meeting, which will include the following items for discussion:

**INITIAL PROJECT MEETING/PRE-START MEETING
SPECIMEN AGENDA**

1 Introduction
2 Project
3 Contract
4 Statutory obligations
5 Health and safety matters
6 Contractual matters
7 Clerk of work's matters
8 Consultants' matters
9 Quantity surveyor's matters
10 Communications and procedures
11 Meetings

Introductions
This is the introduction of the representatives and parties to the contract. Individuals' roles should be clarified and an indication of any specialist appointed by the client for the contract should be given.

Project works

This is a brief description of the project and its principles and objectives and a description of the details of the site and any special restrictions such as access.

Contract

This is when the confirmation of the contract takes place i.e. the exchange of letters between the contractor and client is required and the status with regard to preparation and signature of documents. It is usual to hand over all production information necessary for carrying out the works and review the situation regarding issuing other information. Insurance documents must be viewed and confirmed as valid. It is the landscape architect's/contract administrator's responsibility to ensure that the client receives all necessary evidence to his satisfaction that the contractor is properly insured throughout the course of the contract until the issue of practical completion. The landscape architect/contract administrator should also remind the contractor to check the subcontractor's insurance. The contractor's tax exemption certificate should be checked and the requirement of a bond confirmed or otherwise. At this stage it should be checked that the client has registered with the Health and Safety Executive if required to do so.

Confirmation of the timing for the contract is also necessary, and the date of possession, date of commencement, date of completion and maintenance period times or dates are confirmed.

Statutory obligations

Compliance with statutory requirements regarding noise, safety, building regulations, local by-laws and restrictions, Health and Safety Executive etc. is discussed at this stage.

Health and safety issues

The health and safety plan will be discussed and the planning supervisor will highlight the roles of the individual parties.

Contractor's matters

Note should be made that the work programme supplied by the contractor must be in the form required e.g. bar chart. It must contain adequate separate work elements to measure their progress and integration with service installation, allocate specific dates for nominated subcontract work, relate to landscape architect's instructions and be kept up to date.

Agreement should be reached on site organization, such as location of site compound and facilities, services and access to the site.

Quality control should be discussed to cover the definition of the contractor's duty to supervise, the landscape architect's or contract administrator's duty to inspect and the clerk of works or supervisory staff's duties in connection with the works.

Specialist works require a review of outstanding requirements for information to or from the contractor in connection with specialist works and clarification that the contractor is responsible for co-ordinating specialist works, and for their workmanship and materials.

Other issues such as testing and statutory undertakers should also be discussed at this stage.

Clerk of works' matters
The contractor must provide the clerk of works with adequate facilities as well as all relevant information on site staff, equipment and operations for his weekly reports to the landscape architect. Procedures for quality checks through certificates, vouchers and samples of material, samples of workmanship, test procedures set out in the Bill of Quantities, adequate protection and storage and visits to supplier's/manufacturer's works are discussed.

Consultants' matters
This requires a description of what the consultants are employed to do and confirmation that all instructions are to be issued by the landscape architect/contract administrator. Also a timetable for specialist drawings should be established.

Quantity surveyor's matters/payments
Procedures are to be agreed for valuations in accordance with the client's instructions regarding timing. The percentage retention is to be clarified along with clarification of percentage value of goods and materials to be taken into account.

It is worth confirming that dayworks will only be accepted on written instructions and that day sheets are required within seven days for signature by the landscape architect.

Tax requirements both for the client and contract concerning VAT should be agreed.

Communications and procedures
It should be established that requests for information should be in writing, the landscape architect will respond to queries quickly, technical queries are raised with the clerk of works initially, policy queries and discrepancies are referred to the landscape architect for resolution. All information issued by the contract administrator will be via standard forms and certificates. Distribution and numbers of copies of drawings and instructions required by recipients is to be agreed. Clarification is required that only written instructions from the landscape architect are valid and all oral instructions will be confirmed in writing within 48 hours. The contractor must notify the landscape architect of any written confirmations outstanding. Claims are to be strictly in accordance with the terms of the contract. Any events should be raised immediately the relevant conditions occur.

Meetings
Types of meetings necessary require to be established e.g. progress, site or design team meetings and their frequency.

Progress Meetings

Progress meetings are held to establish the progress of the contractor in relation to his programme. They are also a mechanism for keeping all parties informed of the situation with the contract and any issues arising from the contract. They should be held at regular intervals over the contract period suitable to the length of the contract.

TYPICAL AGENDA FOR PROGRESS MEETING

1 Present
2 Minutes of last meeting
3 Matters arising from last meeting
4 Contractor's progress
   - General report
   - Subcontractor's report
   - Progress and comparison with programme
   - Percentage of main items complete
   - Causes for delay
   - Claims arising
   - Information received since last meeting
   - Information and drawings required, instructions required
5 Clerk of works' report
   - Site matters – weather and general quality control
   - Lost time
6 Consultants' report
7 Quantity surveyor's report
   - Valuation and measurement
   - Updated cost reports
8 Health and safety matters
9 Communication and procedures
   - Drawings issued
   - Meetings held
   - Instructions issued
10 Contract completion date
11 Any other business
12 Date, time and place of next meeting

Definitions

The next few pages describe some of the issues relating to definitions within contract documentation or situations arising from contracts and explain how the various parties deal with them.

Certificates

The Conditions of Contract state that the contract administrator is to issue certificates. There are two types of certificate:

> • **CERTIFICATES OF PAYMENT** •
> • **CERTIFICATES OF PROGRESS** •

Certificates of Payment

> **The Progress Payment Certificate**

The JCLI landscape works contract conditions require a contract administrator to certify progress payments at intervals of not less than four weeks (or at certain specified stages of the work) in respect of the value of the works properly exercised (as agreed by the landscape architect), materials on site and deduction of retention money.

The amount due to the contractor is written on a standard form and a copy is sent to the contractor, quantity surveyor and client. The client must pay within the time specified in the contract.

> **The Penultimate Certificate**

Within 14 days of issuing the certificate of practical completion the landscape architect must issue a penultimate certificate of payment. It is priced on the basis of 97.5 per cent of the contract sum adjusted for the cost of variations, prime cost and provisional sums and any fluctuations to which the contractor is entitled, and the release of half the retention money. The valuation of this certificate must be accurate since the contract does not provide for the issue of any other before the final certificate.

> **The Final Certificate**

Having received from the contractor all the necessary documentation within three months, or the period specified in the contract, of practical completion, the landscape architect must issue a final certificate. This must be issued within 28 days and will cover the balance due to the contractor. The payment should be honoured by the client within the period specified in the contract. The amount specified will include all outstanding monies and the final half of the retention money. It will be issued on a standard form and copied as before.

JCLI Maintenance Certificate of Payment

The JCLI Maintenance Agreement allows for periodic payments to the landscape contractor at intervals of one month. There is no retention but there is a system whereby the client can deduct monies for individual items of work not being carried out or not in accordance with the specification or on time. There is also a bonus that can be added to the contractor's annual certificate if the contractor is performing well.

Certificates of Progress

The Practical Completion Certificate

The contract administrator must certify the date when in his opinion the works have reached practical completion i.e. whether work is sufficiently complete to be safely used for the purpose for which it was designed. There is a standard form for most contracts but with ICE conditions, a letter is issued.

IMPLICATIONS OF PRACTICAL COMPLETION

- All parties know that works are finished.
- The contractor is no longer required to carry insurance for the works.
- The contractor can apply for release of bond.
- The contractor can apply for half retention money.
- The period of final measurement may start.
- The defects liability period begins.

There is also a certificate of non-completion required to start the liquidated and ascertained damages process.

The Certificate of Non-Completion

IMPLICATIONS OF NON-COMPLETION

- All parties know that the works are not complete on the due date.
- The contractor must continue to complete the works.
- Liquidated and ascertained damages can be sought from the contractor.

It is the contract administrator's responsibility to ensure that the planning supervisor has all the information required for health and safety before this certificate is issued.

The Certificate of Making Good Defects

The contractor has to make good any defects both in the hard works and soft works (pre-practical completion) within a specified period after practical completion. The contract administrator has a duty to certify when the contractor has made them good with a certificate of making good defects. If the contractor is responsible for the maintenance of the soft works (post-practical completion) he will be required to make good any defects within a specified time after practical completion. The contract administrator has a duty to certify when the contractor has made them good.

Instructions

A written instruction to proceed with, omit or change any aspect of the works is made provided it is a minor change with small monetary value. It can also be used to omit prime cost and provisional sums. They are issued by the contract administrator on a standard form and must follow a verbal instruction within two days.

Variations

The contract administrator can issue instructions for the following reasons:

A Variation

- The expenditure of a prime cost.
- The expenditure of a provisional sum.
- Any major addition.
- Any major omission or change in the works.
- A major change to the order or period in which the works are to be carried out that is necessary.

If this involves time or money contractually or a by a client's decision it is called a variation. It is issued on the same forms as instructions.

It is the contract administrator's or QS's responsibility to value the variations but usually it is agreed between the landscape architect or QS and the contractor.

VALUING OF VARIATIONS

- The same work under similar conditions at the contract rate and prices.
- Similar work under different conditions based on contract rates.
- Different work for which no rates exist, at fair and reasonable rates.
- Works that cannot be measured at dayworks rates.

Dayworks

Dayworks are used where a specific set of works is to be undertaken which are not included within the original contract documents. A contingency sum is allowed in the documents and can only be expended on written authority of the landscape architect.

Dayworks must always be authorized beforehand and it is important to check that the rates, prices, quantity of labour and materials are correct.

The valuation of work on a daywork basis consists of the actual (prime) cost to the contractor of labour, materials and plant, to which are added his incidental costs, overheads and profit, all expressed as a percentage addition.

The contractor must keep records of amount of labour, time worked and the plant used. The clerk of works keeps a close eye on the works and checks daywork sheets. Daywork sheets should be submitted on a Monday following the work. The landscape architect must approve the daywork sheets.

Bond

A bond is an assurance against the contractor not completing the works. It is taken out by the contractor in the name of the client and the contractor, and placed in a bank account. If the contractor does not perform, the client receives the money. It is written into the contract documents as a sum or percentage.

Retention money

A deduction from each interim certificate of payment is made. The amount is usually 5 per cent of the contract. Half will be given back to the contractor at practical completion, half at the end of the defects liability period.

Liquidated Damages

This is an assessed sum of money that is to be paid by the contractor if he fails to complete the works in the period of time required. It is based on an assessment made by the client of loss due to non-use or non-trading on the site, and written into the contract documents.

- Liquidated: failure to operate i.e. bank loan amount or failure/loss of revenue.
- Ascertained: specific failure i.e. ten car parking spaces × amount per car. It is an exact amount.

Liquidated and ascertained damages can only be applied with a certificate of non-completion. If the contract administrator fails to take off L&A damages, the client is entitled to do so.

Extensions of Time

Contracts provide for the contractor to notify the contract administrator if it becomes apparent the works will not be completed by the contract completion date 'for reasons beyond the control of the contractor'.

In most large building contracts there are 13 relevant events:

REASONS FOR AN EXTENSION OF TIME – JCT

- 'Force majeure'.
- Exceptionally adverse weather conditions.
- Civil commotion.
- Compliance with instructions.
- Opening up work that proved to be satisfactory.
- Late instructions.
- Nominated subcontractor's delay.
- Delay by other contractors or suppliers organized by the employer.
- Statutory powers or reasons beyond the contractor's control affecting the use of labour or securing of goods essential to the works.
- Statutory undertaker's work.
- Prevention of ingress or egress by the employer.
- Postponement of the works by the employer or architect.
- A release schedule by the architect.

In JCLI it is quoted 'for reasons beyond the control of the contractor including compliance of any instruction of the contract administrator whose issue is not due to a default of the contractor'.

The contract administrator must make in writing an extension of the time for completion that is reasonable. (An event that causes delay does not automatically result in an extension, it must cause delay to the critical path of the contract). In addition the landscape architect must ascertain the amount of loss and expense involved to the contractor if notified by the contractor and include it in any progress payments.

Determination

By the client/employer

The client can determine the contractor's employment if the contractor fails to proceed diligently with the works or wholly suspends carrying out the works, or if the contractor becomes bankrupt, makes a composite arrangement with his creditors or has a provisional liquidator appointed or a winding up order made.

In the first situation the employer must give seven days' notice in which he requires the default to be ended. In the case of bankruptcy determination is by notice and is actioned on the date of notice.

Determination is by notice (registered post or recorded delivery) and is actioned on the date of the notice. The date it is received the contractor must cease activities and immediately give up possession of the works. Upon receipt of the notice, determination is immediate. The client may require the contractor to remove his equipment and assign all delivery agreements to any new contractor he employs.

By the contractor

The contractor can determine his own employment if the client fails to make progress payment under the provision of the contract or makes a default with regard to VAT, if the client obstructs the issue of any certificate due, if the client or his representative interferes or obstructs the works or fails to make the site available for the works, if the client suspends the works for a continuous period of one month or if the client goes bankrupt, makes a composite arrangement with his creditors or has a provisional liquidation appointed or a winding up order made.

In the first three situations determination must be by notice (registered post and recorded delivery). This notice specifies the default and requires it to be ended. After receipt of the notice the client has seven days to cease any of the activities described otherwise the contractor will serve further notice to determine the contract. Determination shall take effect on the date of receipt of that notice.

If the client goes bankrupt determination is by notice and it takes effect upon the date of the notice by the client/employer.

WHEN DISASTER STRIKES!
- You must keep the client informed; you must act on their agreement.
- Assess any financial implications of any decision made.

- Set out especially in a dispute to act with balanced judgement and act reasonably.
- Imagine your opinion being put to an arbiter at a later date.
- Act quickly (discuss the matter with colleagues).
- Do not hesitate to bring in outside advice or expertise.
- Keep the fullest possible documentation of your contract.
- Ensure the clarity and precision of the documentation before going to tender; it is important.

Action Following Determination

Determination by Employer

The contractor ceases to occupy the site and the employer may recover additional cost to him for completing the works and any expenses incurred as a direct result of the determination, i.e. consultants' fees, re-tendering or approaching second lowest contractor.

Determination by Contractor

The contractor prepares an account setting out the total value of the work executed and materials on site, costs of removing site equipment and direct loss/damage caused by the determination, and the employer must then pay the contractor the amount due within 28 days of its submission by the contractor.

Index